TO:

_____

FROM:

_____

DATE:

_____

give grace

HOW TO EMBRACE THE BEAUTY OF LIFE'S BROKENNESS

MEGAN SMALLEY

THOMAS NELSON
Since 1798

Give Grace

© 2021 Megan Smalley

Published in Nashville, Tennessee, by Thomas Nelson. Thomas Nelson is a registered trademark of HarperCollins Christian Publishing, Inc.

Thomas Nelson titles may be purchased in bulk for educational, business, fundraising, or sales promotional use. For information, please email SpecialMarkets@ThomasNelson.com.

Scripture quotations taken from The Holy Bible, New International Version®, NIV®. Copyright © 1973, 1978, 1984, 2011 by Biblica, Inc.® Used by permission of Zondervan. All rights reserved worldwide. www.Zondervan.com. The "NIV" and "New International Version" are trademarks registered in the United States Patent and Trademark Office by Biblica, Inc.®

Any Internet addresses, phone numbers, or company or product information printed in this book are offered as a resource and are not intended in any way to be or to imply an endorsement by Thomas Nelson, nor does Thomas Nelson vouch for the existence, content, or services of these sites, phone numbers, companies, or products beyond the life of this book.

ISBN 978-1-4002-1758-8
ISBN 978-1-4002-1756-4 (ebook)
ISBN 978-1-4002-1761-8 (audio)

Printed in China

21 22 23 24 25 DSC 5 4 3 2 1

Contents

Introduction   v

1. We Can Do Hard Things Because God Can
   Do Hard Things   1
2. Grace Through the Storm   13
3. Finding Grace in Pain   27
4. The Grace of Your Story   41
5. Grace-Filled Thoughts   55
6. Grace in Grief   67
7. An Attitude of Grace   83
8. The Grace of Faith   101
9. The Grace of Hope   117
10. Grace in Gratitude   131
11. A Community of Grace   147
12. Grace in Friendship   163
13. Give Grace Freely   177

Conclusion   193

Introduction

For it is by grace you have been saved,
through faith—and this is not from
yourselves, it is the gift of God.
Ephesians 2:8

Welcome, friend. I'm so glad you're here. I'm guessing that if you've opened this book, it's because the concept of grace is tugging at your heart. It does that to me too. Whether life is difficult or easy, deliriously good or downright challenging, roses and sunshine or storm clouds and rain, I constantly feel that pull to grace in my heart. Sometimes it's just the faintest whisper, reminding me to give grace to others and to thank God for the grace He's given me. At other times, it's a roar that overwhelms everything else, mostly in the moments when I am crying out for God's grace to hold me up and keep me going. Whether you are hearing a whisper or a roar, I'm glad you are here to talk about grace with me.

So just what is grace? Grace can mean a lot of different things, but I think the biggest one is that it is the unmerited, but freely given, love, favor, and forgiveness of God. It is Jesus dying on the cross for our salvation. It is the forgiveness of our sins. It is the abundance of blessings God gives to each of us. It is the people who love us in spite of ourselves. It is the opportunities and second, third, and fourth chances we find in life. It is the forgiveness we give one another and ourselves. It is the care and love we show to our communities and to ourselves. It is the Holy Spirit within each of us that leads us to be more like Jesus every day. It is that first step we'll take into heaven, bathed in love and light.

Let's be honest here, none of us is promised an easy road. We all mess up. We all struggle. We all fall short of perfection. We all need grace to make it through, and we all need grace to make it home. Fortunately, God gives us His grace in abundance, like every Christmas and birthday smushed together into one ultimate gift. So if God can give His grace so freely to us, doesn't it make sense that we should be giving grace just as freely, both to ourselves and to others? We need to be throwing grace around like confetti! That's what I want to share with you in this book, the absolute joy of giving grace.

Hi! I'm Megan Smalley. In case you aren't familiar with me, I'm a wife, a mom to three miracle boys, and I will always be a Texas girl at heart, even though I live in Alabama. I'm also the founder and owner of an online clothing shop called Scarlet & Gold. You should check it out! So why is a business owner writing a book about grace? I'm glad you asked! The short answer is that I've been walking a difficult, grief-filled, insanely challenging few years, and through it all, God has been opening my eyes and heart to the beauty and love of His grace. I want to share what I've learned with you, because it is life-changing and life-giving, and I just can't keep that to myself!

I wish I could hear all about your story. Maybe you are trying to figure out how to give grace to someone specific in your life who has hurt you, maybe even broken your heart. Maybe you are trying to find a way to give grace to yourself after a few choices you wish you hadn't made. Or maybe life has just been so darn difficult, and you need all the grace you can get. Whatever you are going through, I promise that the same grace I have experienced is there for you.

The hard stuff we face in life and how we deal with it changes us, shapes us into who we were always meant to be, and becomes the best parts of our stories. I want my story to be one filled to the brim with grace, and I want that for you too. As you read this book, I pray you do so with an open heart, ready to receive God's truth as we dig into what it looks like to understand, receive, and give grace.

In grace,

Megan

ONE

We can do hard things because God can do hard things

———

I will never forget the moment I heard the doctor say the words, "IVF is your only chance to have a baby."

I sat there in that cold office and felt completely numb. I have no idea what else he said to us. His voice just faded away as I stared past him at the drab gray wall with its cheerful posters of reproductive parts (who in the world wants to look at those?) and thought, *This is not my life. This has to be a dream.* I know now that I was in shock. Having a baby was my biggest dream since I got married. I grew up taking care of my younger sisters and had quite the booming babysitting business. I love taking care of others, and I couldn't wait to do that for my kids. I deeply desired to get to experience feeling a little life fluttering and kicking inside of me, giving birth, becoming a mama, snuggling a precious newborn, and raising kids. Being a mom had always felt like a calling on my life. At twenty-seven, I was healthy and exhibited no signs or family history whatsoever of infertility. This was *not* supposed to be my story.

We all have moments in life that are so unexpected, so devastating, and so life-altering that we know that nothing will ever be quite the same from that point forward. A moment when the fire springs up around us and our only choice is to walk through the flames and hope we can make it through without getting burned. That was definitely one of those moments for me. In fact, that was probably the first of those moments I'd ever faced, although more were just waiting for me on the horizon. Have you been there yet? Have you faced something so big and overwhelming to your heart that you aren't sure you are going to make it through?

That day began a four-year journey down a path that I never would have chosen for myself. But isn't that how it happens for most of us? We have our lives all planned out, and then reality yanks the rug out from under our feet with an unrecoverable opportunity, cancelled plans, or an unforeseen tragedy. Our dreams have crumbled to dust, and we are left facing the fire and trying to find our way through. Can I share something with you? There's an absolute truth that I wish I'd known then: God is always in control, and you can trust Him.

Promises From God You Can Count On

"For I am the Lord your God who takes hold of your right hand and says to you, do not fear; I will help you." Isaiah 41:13

Blessed is the one who perseveres under trial because, having stood the test, that person will receive the crown of life that the Lord has promised to those who love him. James 1:12

"My grace is sufficient for you, for my power is made perfect in weakness." Therefore I will boast all the more gladly about my weaknesses, so that Christ's power may rest on me. 2 Corinthians 12:9

We know that in all things God works for the good of those who love him, who have been called according to his purpose. Romans 8:28

God is faithful; he will not let you be tempted beyond what you can bear. But when you are tempted, he will also provide a way out so that you can endure it. 1 Corinthians 10:13

Looking back, God knew exactly what He was doing when He set my feet on that broken road. He knew what I needed. He wanted me to trust Him, to know that He had my back. I wish I could tell you that that's exactly what I did, but it wasn't. Instead of resting in God and allowing Him to lead me through

"I have told you these things,
so that in me you may have peace.
In this world you will have trouble.
But take heart!
I have overcome the world."

John 16:33

the fire, I fought tooth and nail for some semblance of control. I grieved deeply. I was angry that His plans looked different from mine. His plans felt so unfair. I looked side to side and wondered why everyone else was getting the easy road and I had to go through this. I was devastated that we would have to pay tens of thousands of dollars to do something other people do for free all the time! I didn't understand why the biggest desire of my heart was suddenly shut behind a locked door. I convinced myself that God was punishing me for all the sins of my past—yes, even the time I wore my sister's brand-new dress without asking her first, knowing how mad she would be! It was bad.

I refused to believe this was going to be our story. I begged God to change things. I pleaded with Him to take the pain away and to answer our prayers. I did literally everything except to stand on what I believed to be true: That God's plans are always so much better than our plans. That His grace is sufficient at all times and for all things.

Sounds crazy, right? It was. But underneath all the craziness and chaos, God was teaching me something. I might not have had much grace for God and His plans, but He had it in abundance for me. While I was questioning and yelling and doubting, He was whispering His truth into my heart, saying, "Just wait. Just watch. Let Me show you what I have in store for you. It's better than anything you've ever imagined."

It took me a while to hear it and even longer to accept it, but it was worth it. Every tear, every heartbreak, every moment of doubt—they were all worth it because all of that changed me, shaped me, and made me into the woman I am today. The woman who *knows*, deep down in her bones, what I only *believed* before.

Whatever fire you are facing—infertility, career struggles, illness, the loss of one of your people, heartbreak, friendship drama, or just making big decisions for your life—I promise you don't have to walk through it alone. God is with you. He is covering you in His grace. His grace is making you fireproof. He never says that we won't feel the heat, because we will. But what I think we too often forget is that not all fire is destructive. Fire can burn you up, but it can also soften you so you can be reshaped into something new. It can temper you, like metal or glass, making you tougher, stronger, and more beautiful. So yes, when we walk through those flames, we will feel it, but if we lean into the work God is doing, we will come out on the other side changed.

I stand here on the other side of the fire to tell you that you can do hard things. You can! And I'm here to hold your hand through it all and cheer you on as you choose joy and trust and grace, even on the darkest days.

Stop and Reflect

What is the last fire you faced? The last time your plans got totally derailed?

_____
_____
_____
_____
_____
_____
_____
_____
_____

Did you feel angry at God?

When my grandpa
_____
_____
_____
_____
_____
_____
_____
_____

How did walking through that fire change you?

_____

_____

_____

_____

_____

_____

_____

_____

_____

_____

Let's get real for a second. Hard things are the worst! There's no other way to say it. Even knowing what I know now, I still struggle when I find myself in front of the fire again. I know I should say a prayer, take a deep breath, let go of my plans, and step forward bravely. But instead, I always look around first, searching for that shortcut, the easier road, think-ing, *God, I'm good. I've got everything all planned out, thank You very much. I don't need to grow, so I'm just gonna pass on all this hard stuff.* Are you with me? If we were in control of our lives, wouldn't we all choose the easy way if it meant less heartbreak? Of course we would, which is why I'm so thankful that God is the One in charge instead of me.

At my very first Passion Conference, a Christian conference for college students, I heard Francis Chan speak. He told a story about a time when he preached a sermon and afterward someone told him that he looked refreshed. As Chan walked away, he thought to himself that he didn't want to look refreshed. He didn't want his life to be so easy that he had plenty of time to be refreshed. He wanted to look tired and worn down because he had been busy fighting a battle for God. He wanted to spend all of his time fighting bravely and boldly for the kingdom. So he began praying that God would bring him battles to fight. He didn't pray for God to take *away* struggles from his life; he prayed for God to *give* him battles and the endurance to overcome and persevere. Wow.

I knew in my heart that I have never been brave enough to utter such a prayer. But I wanted to be. What would my life look like if I had that attitude? What if I welcomed hard things with open arms because I was so ready to put on the armor of God and fight? Those battles, the hard things, more than anything else in life, help us become who we were always meant to be. The fact that we are able to learn and grow and change and become wiser through hard things is a privilege. It's a chance for our faith to become deeper as we strive every day to become more like Jesus—I mean, whoa, right? What a gift. Those hard things that give us that gift, well, I'd say they are a form of grace too. One I'm very thankful for.

Let's Pray

Heavenly Father,

Thank You for the battles You have given me to fight, both big and small. I am grateful for the opportunity to learn and grow. I know that I'm not in this fight alone. Thank You for staying beside me and giving me Your strength to lean on. I'm ready if You have more battles for me. Help me to be brave, bold, and tireless as I persevere through the fire.

In Jesus' name, amen.

TWO

Grace through the storm

—

I'm not going to pretend that I felt anything close to being brave, bold, and tireless as I found myself facing my first big battle. When I heard that doctor tell us that IVF was our only option to ever have biological kids, I was devastated by grief and anxiety. Instead of focusing on the hope and grace I have in God and His ability to bring me through any crisis, I let my imagination run away with me completely. I imagined every worst-case scenario in the book and a few that absolutely have no basis in reality at all. I let my emotions overwhelm me, and I swung from anger to sadness to jealousy to fear to grief to hope all day, every day. It was exhausting. But I think this is fairly normal when we run up against something we can't control, right? I couldn't control the situation, so I let the situation control me.

In the summer of 2014, Blake and I decided to pursue IVF at a local clinic. We were told we'd be a slam-dunk case, so our hearts were full of hope. But it was still a huge risk. There are no guarantees with IVF, and there is no refund if you don't end up pregnant. We drained our savings account for one shot at having a baby. I felt guilty and scared and a little bit (okay, a lot!) desperate. I was asking God for a miracle, but I still didn't fully trust Him enough to hand over control. Instead, I drove myself and everyone around me crazy trying to do everything perfectly leading up to our transfer. I got my nurse friends to help me with my medicine and shots. I set a timer so I wouldn't be late by even a minute with my doses. I was early for every blood draw and ultrasound. I read every article and book I could find and did everything they suggested. But after our only three embryos were transferred, I still wasn't pregnant.

All of that striving, all of that research, all of that money and it amounted to nothing. An empty womb and broken hearts. We didn't have the money to try again, and even if we had, I'm not sure I would have survived another round approaching it like I did. We spent the next year of our lives trying to recover physically, emotionally, and financially as we watched so many of our friends get pregnant. Every time another friend shared her happy news with me, it was like someone was ripping off the Band-Aids I had worked so hard to put on my heart. I was happy for them, but I was sad for us. How could I explain to them that my tears are full of both grief and joy—grief over my story and joy for theirs?

So I hid a lot that year while I grieved. Facing people was difficult because I didn't want to answer questions and I didn't want to hear the unsolicited advice. I didn't want to be asked what our plan was because we didn't have a plan.

No one is cast off
by the Lord forever...
He will show compassion.

Lamentations 3:31–32

If this is where you are in your story—staring down a dark, uncertain path, unsure if you even have the courage to take the next step, please don't give up. Does the road feel lonely? Are you looking around and it seems like everyone else is living different, better lives? Lives full of dreams achieved and plans working out flawlessly? Lives full of productivity and joy and ease? And yet here you are, feeling left behind in a puddle of disappointment. Comparison, doubt, shame, fear, and anxiety can consume your mind and your heart as you wait and wait and wait for it to finally be your turn. You feel stuck.

That was me for four years. If I could go back in time and talk to the me then, living in that stuck time, I would give her the biggest hug and then tell her to give herself grace. I would tell her to give herself grace in her grief and to cry when she needs to. I would encourage her to give herself grace in the blame game she's been playing and forgive herself for her past mistakes and messes (which have nothing to do with her infertility).

I would tell her to give herself grace in her loneliness and that it is okay to share her pain with her friends instead of pretending to be strong. I would encourage her to give grace to those same friends, the ones who love her but don't know how to help, what to say, or who say all the wrong things. I would repeat it over and over again until she listened. Grace. Grace. Grace. Grace. Because if she had known then what I know now, she would have seen that she wasn't stuck; she was preparing while she waited. She was taking tiny baby steps that the world could see, but gigantic leaps in her heart and soul.

Stop and Reflect

If you could talk to a past version of yourself who was struggling, what would you say?

_____

_____

_____

_____

_____

_____

How would you offer grace to your past self?

_____

_____

_____

_____

_____

_____

_____

What would you tell her to give her hope?

_____

_____

_____

_____

_____

_____

Two years later, God covered me in the kind of grace only He can offer. My wonderful team at Scarlet & Gold helped put together a fundraising campaign that became known as the Give Grace campaign to give us the opportunity we desperately longed for. They designed products to sell and paid for them to be produced so that one hundred percent of the profit went toward our fertility treatments. We were given the answer to our prayers, one more chance to try IVF. We transferred our two best embryos on December 14, 2016. This time joy replaced grief, and we welcomed our twin boys, Elijah and Stisher (it's a family name), on August 8, 2017. Raising twins has been a challenge in a whole new way, but we have been able to face parenthood with a grace-filled perspective. When uncertainty, doubt, and fear pop up, we are able to look at our boys and remember that God's plans are always better than ours.

May we shout for joy over your victory and lift up our banners in the name of our God.

Psalm 20:5

Whatever you are walking through, God already reigns victorious. If we keep our eyes on Jesus and not on our circumstances, He will give us peace in the midst of the storm. It's a daily battle to take our eyes off our circumstances and refocus our hearts and minds on Jesus. On the days when you feel you can't take another step, tell Him. He will meet you in those vulnerable moments to give you peace and strength to keep moving forward. He's not scared of your mess. Be honest about where you're struggling, and trust that He will be the hand you can always cling to, the One who never leaves your side. The truth is that you are never alone, especially during your most heartbreaking moments.

A verse that captures where God is in our toughest moments that I come back to over and over again comes from Isaiah 43:2: "When you pass through the waters, I will be with you; and when you pass through the rivers, they will not sweep over you. When you walk through the fire, you will not be burned; the flames will not set you ablaze." When we hit those moments we never imagined would be in the pages of our stories, it *feels* like drowning or walking through fire, doesn't it? God promises to be with us in the roughest waters. Isn't that beautiful?

Infertility felt like way more than I could handle. There were many days I wouldn't have been able to get out of bed without Jesus because grief consumed me. The sadness felt like a dark cloud looming over me, like a ton of bricks piled on my chest, pressing the life out of me. In those moments, I had to remind myself of God's promises. In those moments, I read Ephesians 3:20–21 over and over and reminded myself that God is able: "Now to him who is able to do immeasurably more than all we ask or imagine, according to his power that is at work within us, to him be glory in the church and in Christ Jesus throughout all generations, for ever and ever! Amen." If I truly believed that He is able and He is who He says He is, I had to choose to put my feet on the ground and take one step forward at a time, knowing God was by my side. I had to choose to tell myself I could do hard things because He can do all the hard things.

Give Yourself Grace

When you are facing hard things and you feel overwhelmed, here are some ideas for how you can give yourself grace and rest:

- Put down your phone. Take a break from social media. All the noise of other people's lives can lead to comparison and shame when you are struggling. Use that time instead to read a great book, spend time with your people, or pray.

Go for a walk outside in nature. Listen to the sounds of God's creation, and let the beauty around you calm your soul.

Be kind to your body. Eat good, wholesome food. Exercise. Sleep. When your body is healthy, your mind will follow.

Read your Bible. Go straight to the Source and immerse yourself in the grace in God's Word.

I believe the hard things in our lives show us how much we need God. If we didn't face these difficulties, we'd all be much less dependent on God because we'd start to believe that we were okay on our own. But if we don't need God, this whole salvation thing means nothing, and I *know* that's all wrong. Salvation is *everything*.

There's a wonderful podcast episode by Nancy Ray titled *You Were Made for Hard Things*. At the end of one episode, she gives a powerful illustration about cows, buffalo, and storms. Did you know that when cows see a storm coming on the horizon, they run as fast as they can away from the storm? You'd think that after living through several storms, they'd realize that this isn't the best option. Because no matter how fast they run, the storm will eventually catch them. And when

When the storm
has swept by,
the wicked are gone,
but the righteous
stand firm forever.

Proverbs 10:25

it does, they will be exhausted from running, and the storm feels twenty times worse than it actually is.

But buffalo are a little bit more clever. When they see a storm coming, they run directly at it. They charge the storm, unafraid, understanding that if they run through it, the storm will pass over them and it will all be over so much faster. Almost all of us default to cow-behavior. Moo! We run from the storm because we are so afraid of it. We end up running ourselves empty, and we have no strength left to face the storm when it reaches us. How do you want to face the storm? I'd like to face my storms like a buffalo. I believe that when we let go of fear and trust God to get us through, we'll move through life's storms so much more quickly. He will supply us with the grace and the strength to endure it for as long as it lasts.

Let's Pray

Father God,

I know I can do hard things with You. Please help me to remember that each and every day. Please bring me the other hard things You think I need. Hold my hand and help me be brave enough to run toward those storms.

In Your Son's name, amen.

THREE

Finding grace in pain

—

One of the biggest parts of giving ourselves grace is that we must, must, must allow ourselves to feel our feelings and grieve our losses. When you look around at success stories in our culture, they are often about how someone faced something difficult and put aside their feelings and grief so that they could overcome. I see those stories and think, *Well there's a recipe for disaster after the fact.* Putting aside your feelings doesn't make them go away. Those feelings will still have to be felt and dealt with, and the longer you put them off, the worse it will be!

Here's the thing, God has already overcome the world. We don't need to divorce ourselves from our feelings to overcome. We don't need to shove our feelings way down to triumph. And God doesn't want us to! God acknowledges that we need to grieve. He also promises that He will one day turn that grief into joy. Grieving when we need to and processing our feelings in healthy ways doesn't make us weak. On the contrary, it makes us stronger and draws us closer to God.

While I was going through my second round of IVF, I had *all* the feelings. The cocktail of hormones my doctor gave me

"Now is your time of grief,
but I will see you again
and you will rejoice, and no one
will take away your joy."

John 16:22

plus the fear and uncertainty I felt knowing that this time could be a failure as well basically turned me into a walking emotional roller coaster. And these weren't my normal feelings—oh no!—these feelings were stronger and more intense than just about anything I'd ever experienced before. As much as I tried to be brave and put on a happy face, there were so many moments when I cried over nothing. Processing all of those emotions took up a lot of my energy on a daily basis. I spent so much time praying, constantly reminding myself to trust God.

A few weeks away from my scheduled embryo transfer, I had just enough time for a quick trip home. Seeing my family was what I so desperately needed. It was Thanksgiving, a time that felt extra special in the midst of so much uncertainty and possible heartbreak. While I was there, my younger sister, Mallory, and I decided to drive to Waco to visit our baby sister, Becca, for a few days of sister time.

Mallory and I were halfway to Waco when she turned off the music and said, "I have something I need to tell you."

My stomach plummeted. Somehow, I just knew exactly what she was going to say, and I also knew that my heart couldn't handle it right then.

"I'm pregnant," she whispered. Her words suddenly so big that they took up all of the space and air in the car.

A wave of grief washed over me in the most literal way. I

couldn't breathe. I felt like a I was being squeezed into nothingness. I wanted to get out of that car as fast as I could because I couldn't even begin to process it all. I knew I should be happy for her, and somewhere inside of me I *was*, but grief over my own story consumed me in that moment.

THE ANGER TRAP

We all need to feel our feelings. This should be instinctual, right? *Sigh*. Sadly, most of us have trained ourselves not to feel our most difficult feelings—sadness, grief, disappointment, betrayal, and shame. Those feelings are uncomfortable to sit with. They make us feel small and low and terribly insignificant. Instead, we have a tendency to turn those feelings into anger. Anger is more acceptable in our society. It spurs us to action and ignites change within us. Anger is familiar. But anger is missing something crucial. Anger is missing grace.

Those other feelings, the ones we keep turning into anger, they are important too. Our feelings are a crucial warning system that tells us when something in our lives is wrong or hurting us. If we don't allow ourselves to sit with those difficult emotions and do the work to look within ourselves and discover where those feelings are coming from, we miss out on the chance for healing.

The next time you find yourself angry, I want to challenge you to go somewhere quiet, get comfy, close your eyes, and really examine why you feel angry. I promise that if you really get honest with yourself, you'll find that 99 percent of the time you are angry you feel disappointed, betrayed, shamed, or somehow less than. Once you identify what you are really feeling, you can start the difficult work of addressing what or who made you feel that way and, hopefully, fix the real issue!

I would have given *anything* in that moment to be able to push my pain aside and be able to express my happiness and excitement for my sister (I'm sure she wished I could have done that too—talk about an awkward car ride!). But the truth is that I was in the middle of one heck of a pity party with lots of extra hormones thrown in, and I had no room in there for anything except my grief.

Now, let me be clear here. There is a difference between processing your feelings in a healthy way and throwing yourself a pity party. Processing your feelings is a generous act of grace for yourself. It involves letting yourself feel, grieve, and pray, all while making progress toward accepting your circumstances as they are. That doesn't mean you can't plan and pursue changes in your circumstances—you absolutely should! And you will as soon as you are done dealing with your emotions.

In contrast, you know when you are throwing yourself a pity party because you'll find yourself wallowing in your feelings. Instead of dealing with your personal issues, you'll focus on comparing your messy life to everyone else's polished, picture-perfect Instagram feed. It's easy to believe that the grass is greener somewhere else. And, if we aren't careful, all that comparison can cause bitterness and resentment and make us blind to the bounty of blessings that we *do* have in our lives. When you are your own walking pity party, you can't give grace to anyone else. Even worse, it can make it next to impossible to trust God and His plans for you.

Whew! I have been there, girl. And here's what I've learned. The only way to get back on the path to joy and contentment despite your circumstances is confronting the pain. It's time to get really honest about everything you are walking through, what you are feeling, and *why* you feel that way. The why is really important. If you can't identify why you feel the way you do, then you can't heal the wound.

When it came to my reaction to Mallory's pregnancy, my *why* ended up surprising me. After all, a lot of my friends became pregnant during my four-year infertility journey. But most of their announcements didn't leave me in a state of pure devastation like Mallory's did. What I realized, after a lot of soul searching, is that my reaction had more to do with my sense of self and identity than it did with Mallory herself. In

Fools give full
vent to their rage,
but the wise bring
calm in the end.

Proverbs 29:11

Put on the new self,
created to be like God
in true righteousness
and holiness.

Ephesians 4:24

our family, I've always been the trailblazer, the leader, and the one who took care of everyone else. So much of who I am has been wrapped up in figuring everything out first and then helping my siblings walk the path I made for them. But this time, I'd been trying and trying and trying for years to make a path through the wilderness, only to find myself utterly stuck. And here was Mallory, walking right past me and easily creating her own path where I had failed.

That might sound ridiculous to you, but Mallory becoming the first of my siblings to have a baby shifted our family dynamics in a big way. I didn't know how to let her go first with grace. I didn't know how to abdicate my role as the big sister who always takes care of her siblings. And she didn't know how to go first and help me because I'd never let her. But, man oh man, did she shine at blazing the trail for both of us.

Mallory delivered her sweet baby boy, Ford, in July, and four weeks later, my boys were born. Looking back now, I get chills because of the *rightness* of the story God orchestrated. He knew that I needed to let go of an identity that I had outgrown so that I could fully embrace my new identity as a mother. My siblings needed that too, so they could grow into their own adult identities. Growing out of something that no longer fits can certainly be painful, but through the pain, God brings beauty. Through the pain, God brings healing. In my case, God ushered Mallory and me into a new stage of our relationship, helping us move further into equality and a deeper friendship. Mallory led the way into motherhood and then, with grace, reached back her hand and helped me along the path, showing me more clearly that my only true identity (one I can *never* outgrow) is the one I find in Jesus.

Stop and Reflect

Is there an identity you're holding on to that might not be serving you anymore?

_____

_____

_____

_____

_____

_____

Are there feelings that you haven't dealt with regarding your circumstances?

_____

_____

_____

_____

_____

Do you know why you are having those feelings?

_____

_____

_____

_____

Are you dealing with your feelings in a healthy way or having a pity party for one?

_____

_____

_____

_____

I am so thankful for how God wrote this story. If I'd had my boys when I wanted, they would have been four years old when Mallory's son was born. Just enough older to make closeness unlikely. I would have been a pro mom by that point, and Mallory would have taken my recommendations and run with them, as per usual. Instead, our boys get to grow up together and nurture lifelong friendships that will be so valuable as time goes on. Mallory got to do the research and figure stuff out and find a new confidence in herself and strength as a mom. She told me which products to buy. She learned what worked and shared that with me. Heck, she even sent me pumped milk when I was having trouble producing enough milk for two babies. If that's not grace and sisterhood all rolled into one, then I just don't know what is!

Having two newborns at one time and a husband who worked long hours was so much harder than I ever could have imagined. Those days were exhausting and sometimes lonely, but there were times that also healed my heart in the biggest ways. I could not have survived those early days if Mallory hadn't gone first and helped me out because I didn't have the emotional, physical, or mental energy to figure things out on my own. Mallory is one of the very best moms I know and watching her with Ford and now Luke is a strong, steady, constant reminder to me that God is faithful and that His plans trump my plans every time.

Let's Pray

Heavenly Father,

Help me to process my feelings in a healthy way and avoid pity parties. Please grant me the wisdom to get to the root of my feelings so I can find healing and resolution. Remind me to give myself grace as I do the work to deal with difficult emotions and even more difficult circumstances. Thank You for allowing me to find my identity in You.

In Christ's name, amen.

FOUR

The grace of your story

——

I have been incredibly privileged. I grew up a pastor's kid at a huge church in Houston, Texas. I was raised in a Christian home by two incredibly loving parents who worked very hard to provide everything we could possibly need. I have two beautiful sisters and a big brother whom I adore. We weren't rich, but we had everything we needed and then some. The greatest struggle I endured in my childhood was occasionally feeling left out by my wealthier classmates. I did a lot of comparing and wishing I had more cash to burn as one of the "staff kids" at my very affluent, private Christian school. (Thankfully, other than the uncanny ability to spot a pair of designer jeans from a mile away, I graduated thankful and very aware of how good I had it!) And then there was college, where my biggest heartbreak was not making the cheerleading squad at Auburn the first time I tried out. Total first-world problems, right?

When your life has been easy and, dare I say, #blessed, those small heartbreaks, tiny setbacks, and minor inconveniences can easily loom terribly large in your mind. It took having to climb some real mountains to show me that all I'd ever seen before were small hills. I was clueless and entitled, and I'm grateful that my friends who had already dealt with some serious tough stuff gave me heaps of grace when I griped to them about my small problems. There's an old saying that "you don't know what you don't know," and that was 100 percent me. I just had no clue what it actually meant to walk through something difficult.

In 2010 that all changed. My baby sister was diagnosed with an eating disorder. Over the span of a few months, we watched as she literally disappeared before our eyes, physically and emotionally. It is absolutely brutal to watch someone you know and love get lost in a disease like that. Fast forward to 2011. Three months after my wedding, my parents checked my older brother into rehab for alcohol and substance addiction.

It was crushing. I can't tell you how many times I wondered if I had done something that caused those issues. It's pretty human to want answers, but sometimes there just aren't any. My siblings and I are close. More than just brothers and sisters, we've always been friends. Suddenly, I felt like I was losing them, and there was so little I could do to help. These weren't childhood bullies I could intimidate for them. These weren't hurt feelings I could soothe away by reading a book or playing their favorite games. These were battles that they really had to fight themselves. There was nothing I could do except remind them that I loved them and pray.

Then in 2013, we found ourselves in the midst of our infertility battle. I already felt worn down from my family's other struggles when I got the news that having biological children would be almost impossible. I think that is part of the reason my grief was so profound. Have you ever felt like that? Like waves of struggle keep sweeping you off of your feet and carrying you out to sea, away from solid ground? Like there is no time to come up for air? Those years of uncertainty, doubt, fear, and heartbreak left my whole family feeling like Noah in his ark, adrift with no land in sight.

But even in the midst of all of that darkness, there was always a light. Each time another wave hit, I was faced with a decision. Do I believe God is who He says He is? Do I believe His promises are true? And if I say I do, how does that look in my life? Does my life match what I say I believe?

Doubt crept in. Fear crept in. Shame crept in. I realized I needed a new game plan. I had been assuming life would be easy and good with only a few struggles peppered in. But that is not what God promises in the Bible. We aren't promised easy or good. In James 1:2, James says, "Consider it pure joy, my brothers and sisters, whenever you face trials of many kinds." Not *if*, but *when*. I realized that I would always be mad and frustrated and feel resentful toward God if I kept believing that struggles were going to be rare. I needed to embrace the idea that there would always be struggles. I needed to look at my

When the dove returned
to him in the evening,
there in its beak was a
freshly plucked olive leaf!
Then Noah knew that the water
had receded from the earth.

Genesis 8:11

story not as a "happily ever after" situation, but as an ongoing series of battles that, handled with faith, would grow and shape me to be more like Jesus. So that also meant that I needed to reframe the concept of grace in my mind.

Since struggles are a constant, that means that grace needs to be a constant as well. You may be thinking, "well, duh!" at this point, but this really was a revolutionary concept to me. I had been thinking of grace as a one-time shot to be doled out as the situation demanded. Wrapping my head around the need for a constant, ever-present stream of grace was trickier than I expected. In fact, it was easier to accept a future filled with struggle than it was to accept a future filled with grace. Crazy, right?

I think we all struggle so much with grace because, deep down, we all feel like we don't deserve it. God doles it out with abandon, but we get so caught up in our shame and guilt and embarrassment that we keep our arms closed, refusing to accept His generous gift. If you were to write your story right now, what words would you use to describe yourself? How do you think God would write your story? Would it look and sound the same coming from Him? My guess is that your answer to that last question is a resounding no! When God writes our stories, He infuses them with grace and love. So why is it so difficult for us to do the same thing?

There is so much unnecessary shame that accompanies

words like *eating disorder, addiction, infertility,* and all of those other words we use during the hardest, most trying times. Those words taste like struggle, like brokenness, like failure. Not exactly words you want to claim as your own, right? I was so scared at first to share my infertility journey. I could just picture the horrible things that people might say or think of me. What if they only saw my infertility and stopped seeing *me?* But attaching broken, failure-laden words to ourselves isn't grace. Words and names have power, and we can choose which words to use when we tell our own stories. Choosing our words carefully is a form of grace that we see over and over again in the Bible.

God's Words for His Children

The Bible is full of stories of the faithful people who have followed God imperfectly. They have all messed up and made mistakes, but God does not call them failures. Instead, He called them:

- Friends (1 John 4:7–8)

- Faithful (Genesis 5:22)

- Highly favored (Luke 1:28)

A man after God's own heart (1 Samuel 13:14)

A chosen people (1 Peter 2:9)

Treasured possessions (Deuteronomy 7:6)

Children of God (1 John 3:1)

Mine (Malachi 3:17)

Heirs of the Kingdom (James 2:5)

Prophet to the nations (Jeremiah 1:5)

How would you see yourself differently if you called yourself these names with God's grace?

In the very beginning, God gave Adam naming rights over all of the animals. It was an important job that He trusted Adam with. Right there in the first book of the Bible, God makes it clear that names matter. Then there are the stories of Abraham and Peter, who both took up new names to signify their commitment to God when He called them. But my favorite is the story of Jacob. Instead of choosing to call the suffering of losing his wife what it was, Jacob recognized that there was power in a name. Rachel had named her son Ben-Oni, meaning "son of my trouble," with her dying breath. Jacob renamed him Benjamin, meaning "son of my right hand." Jacob chose to speak life over his circumstances and over his son. He called it a blessing, joy, hope, and a privilege.

Stop and Reflect

What positive label do you want to give yourself?

_____

_____

_____

_____

_____

_____

_____

_____

_____

_____

_____

_____

_____

_____

Is there a failure or struggle that you want to rename in a positive way?

_____

_____

_____

_____

_____

_____

_____

_____

How can you transform your negative attitude into a positive one, even during trying circumstances?

_____

_____

_____

_____

_____

_____

_____

_____

God's love has been poured out into our hearts through the Holy Spirit, who has been given to us.

Romans 5:5

For a long time, I was consumed with how I'd chosen to label my life and myself. I told myself daily that my life was the pits. I complained that it was frustrating. I whined that it was depressing. I was convinced that my life was nothing but grief, uncertainty, pain, and hopelessness. I lived in that space of negativity, choosing to speak negative words over my circumstances that, in turn, reflected back on my life.

We are not in control of most things that happen in our lives. We want health, but we are handed a life-threatening illness. We want financial security, but we can't find a job in our field. We want marriage, but we find ourselves single. We want to make our flight on time, but an accident delays us. None of those things are what we would have picked, and we can't control them, but we can control our attitudes about and our responses to our circumstances.

I learned the hard way that my negative words and attitude were not the way to give myself grace. So now when I'm challenged, I take the time I need to process or grieve the situation, and then I act on the naming rights I've been given. I choose to shift my attitude, to lean into what God is teaching me, to open my eyes to the blessings in my life, and to give this circumstance a positive name. And you can too. You can take the label you've given yourself or that others have tried to put on you, and you can change it. You can take back your naming rights. Attitude is a choice we must make every single day, sometimes multiple times a day.

Let's Pray

Father God,

Help me to choose positivity and grace today. Help me speak to myself the way that You would speak to me. Thank You for Your Word that I can turn to whenever I need a reminder of Your grace for me.

In Jesus' name, amen.

FIVE

Grace-filled thoughts

—

The waiting between IVF sessions sometimes felt like torture. I wanted to be a mother so badly. It was truly the deepest desire of my heart, and it felt so terribly far away. To make matters worse, most of my friends were also excited to become mothers and it seemed so easy for them. For a while it felt like I was bombarded by pregnancy announcements, gender reveal parties, baby shower invitations, and (the most painful!) those adorable pictures of newborns each month showing how they had grown and changed. I honestly was so proud of my friends and so filled with joy at seeing them become mothers. But, oh, how my heart ached for a baby of my own.

Here I was stuck, deeply desiring something that I felt God had placed on my heart. But as each door shut in my face, I began to question if the desire to have a baby was truly from God. Was I wrong to want this so much?

Nope. I wasn't wrong to desire a baby, and you aren't wrong to desire your dream job or a spot at the school you've hoped to attend. You aren't wrong for desiring a husband and a strong marriage or a cute, little house in that dream neighborhood. God created us to have desires, and He wants us to pray about them and share our dreams with Him. People love to quote Psalm 37:4, which says, "Take delight in the LORD, and he will give you the desires of your heart." That sounds nice and easy, doesn't it? We want something, so all we have to do is delight in God and He'll give it to us, right? But that's not quite how it works. Sometimes God says yes! Other times He says no, or He might say wait. *Wait* and *no* are hard answers to wrestle with.

In Psalm 37:4, the verse doesn't confirm *when* or *how* God will give you the desires of your heart. We have to be willing to trust God that He will give us those desires on His time and in His way or that He will change our hearts. But that can be so dang hard, right? If you are like me, then hearing "wait" is even worse than getting a flat-out no. Instant gratification is where it's at if I'm being 100 percent honest. But that is rarely God's way.

I knew early on in our struggle that it mattered to me how I walked this trial out. I desperately wanted to wait on God well, but there were many days when doubt and fear got the best of me. In the middle of the valley, when I couldn't see that one day I'd hold my own babies in my arms, I had to learn how to keep my heart in check, my thoughts under control, and refocus my eyes on Jesus.

What really helped me was to stay in the Word daily. I

Be still before the LORD and wait patiently for him.

Psalm 37:7

found this practice vital. I had to choose Jesus every morning by filling my mind and my heart with biblical truths. Reading God's Word helped me balance hoping for the things I wanted while giving me a deeper understanding and acceptance that His answer might be no for us. I prayed often. Some days, it felt like I was continually praying and talking to God in my head all day long. I prayed about our choices and our plans— was IVF the right move? Should we be looking at adoption? Should we be content with just the two of us and stop pursuing treatment all together?

I also did my best to give myself the grace to change my mind. I know that seems crazy, since I said that having a baby was the deepest desire of my heart. But I think part of living with grace means keeping our hearts open to change. If our answer was no, then I had to be open to letting God change my deepest desire to match His deepest desire for me. I sat with my grief, and I really thought through our motivations. Why did I want a baby so badly? Was it because our friends were all having them? Were we trying to make our marriage better by adding a kid to the mix? Were we trying to fill a God-shaped hole in our hearts? For me, I truly wanted to be a mother. Examining my motives helped me to feel confident in holding onto my desire. If you strip away all the mess, are you able to be honest about your desires and where they're coming from?

Stop and Reflect

What is the deepest desire of your heart?

_____

_____

_____

_____

_____

Have you looked at the motivations behind that desire?

_____

_____

_____

_____

_____

How do you see God going about granting that desire?

_____

_____

_____

_____

_____

When you are in a period of waiting, it can be so tempting to try to take control of the situation and force a solution. I often thought about the story of Abraham, Sarah, and Hagar. Even though God had clearly told Sarah the promises for her future child, she was sick and tired of waiting. So she took matters into her own hands and told Abraham to have a baby with Hagar. As much as I want to judge Sarah for that choice, I can *so* relate to her desperation. Waiting on God is hard, and she waited a whole lot longer than I did! But taking control isn't grace. Thinking you can do better than God can isn't grace. There is so much beautiful grace in the concept of surrender. Surrendering your desires, your heart, and your plans to God is living in grace, trusting that His desires and His plans for you are the ones you really want.

A PRAYER FOR WHEN YOU ARE WAITING

Dearest God,

Please be with me today during this time of waiting. Help me to keep my eyes and thoughts focused on You. Help me to desire what You desire for me. Help me to live in surrender and grace as I wait, so that I don't miss the beauty and joy and blessings all around me.

In Your name, amen.

When you are living in surrender, it becomes easier to check your attitude. I had to check mine a lot! It wasn't just feelings of sadness or anger I had to watch out for, it was also spiraling thoughts. My imagination is a powerful thing and it led me on a lot of wild goose chases as I imagined worst-case scenarios and let myself get sucked into them emotionally. Do you know what I'm talking about? Maybe your sister leaves you an innocent enough voicemail, and she just says, "Hey, sis, call me when you can." And you call her back, but she doesn't answer. So now you think something is terribly wrong, and by the time she calls you back to ask if she can borrow your navy dress, you've diagnosed her with a life-threatening disease in your mind and you're in tears because you aren't sure you're going get to say good-bye. Okay, so that example is a bit dramatic, but, honestly, most of the scenarios I imagine for myself usually are. What can I say? My imagination is permanently set on worst-case scenario!

It's next to impossible to live in grace when you are always imagining the worst. We have to stop these thoughts before they spiral. Second Corinthians 10:5 says, "We demolish arguments and every pretension that sets itself up against the knowledge of God, and we take captive every thought to make it obedient to Christ." We have to start taking our thoughts captive and filling our minds with truth. You can also take your thoughts captive by speaking life to yourself and your circumstances. It all starts with the mind: a conscious choice to know and stand on what is true, even before your heart fully believes it.

So what is exactly true? The truth is that God never promised me a baby. He never promised me a husband. He never promised me a job or home or family who loves me unconditionally. These are all blessings and gifts God has given me. But His answer could have been no to all of these things. God does not promise us success or *everything* that we want, but He does promise to be with us in the storm. One of my favorite reminders is in Joshua 1:9: "Have I not commanded you? Be strong and courageous. Do not be afraid; do not be discouraged, for the LORD your God will be with you wherever you go."

The best way I overcome the fear and my need to control is to look back on my life and remind myself of all the ways that God has proven Himself to be faithful. Scripture tells us clearly who God is. Numbers 23:19 says, "God is not human, that he should lie, not a human being, that he should change his mind. Does he speak and then not act? Does he promise and not fulfill?" There are many names of God, and through each one, He reveals Himself to us. Simply knowing and understanding the names of God equips us to face hard things because we know who He is and what He promises to do.

The Names of God

I want to encourage you to read the verses below and dig into the meanings of these names. Imprint them on your heart. When God tells us who He is, we should listen and trust Him.

- Jehovah (Exodus 3:13–15)

- Jehovah-M'Kaddesh (Leviticus 20:7–8)

- Jehovah-jireh (Genesis 22:9–14)

- Jehovah-shalom (Judges 6:16–24)

- Jehovah-rophe (Exodus 15:22–26)

- Jehovah-nissi (Exodus 17:8–15)

- El-Shaddai (Genesis 49:22–26)

- Elohim (Genesis 17:7–8)

Trust is an act of faith. It requires a choice on your part to walk by faith and not by sight. Sometimes it can feel strange to put every ounce of hope into a relationship with Someone you've never seen face-to-face. Is that something you struggle with? Trusting in God and in His promises was hard for me for a long time and still sometimes is. But that's where faith comes in, and the more we remind ourselves of who God is and what He has done in our lives and the lives of those around us, the more confidently we can stand on His promises because there's no doubt in our hearts that they are true and that God is real.

Let's Pray

Dear Lord,

Thank You for being who You are. Thank You for sharing Your names and promises with us. Help me to focus on those truths when my mind tries to carry me away.

In Your Son's name, amen.

SIX

Grace in grief

I landed in Denver with a heart full of anticipation. After two years of waiting and raising money, Blake and I were ready for the next step in our journey to a baby. We were about to spend a full day at the world-renowned Colorado Center for Reproductive Medicine for more testing before our next attempt at IVF. I spent the day getting ultrasounds, having tubes upon tubes of blood drawn, and going through lots of other tests. We finally sat down with Dr. Schoolcraft, the brilliant doctor I had read so much about, to review and discuss the test results.

We were hopeful he'd give us good news and say that we would be a slam dunk case. But he didn't. He used words like *uterine blood flow* and *surgery* and *more appointments*. He was cautiously optimistic, but there were several hurdles between us and bringing a baby home. I only heard bits and pieces of what he said because I was once again in shock. I had been so hopeful, so convinced that our last failure was a fluke and that this time would be straightforward and successful.

I felt the emotions rising up in my throat. I couldn't breathe. It felt like someone was sitting on my chest. I left Blake with the doctor and practically ran out of the clinic. I got in the car, cranked up the worship music, and immediately burst into tears. I couldn't hold it in. I had to let it out and allow the grief to wash over me. Not only were we having to do IVF again, which is already basically the worst-case scenario in the fertility treatment world, but we had travelled across the country to see the best-of-the-best doctor. And it still wasn't a guarantee. It was still a huge gamble to move forward with trying to have a baby. In that moment, it all just felt horribly unfair and crushing. I needed to grieve.

Now you may be thinking, *Calm down, Megan, no one died. Grief* is kind of a dramatic word for feeling disappointed, isn't it? Nope, it's exactly the right word for this situation. Let's talk about what grief actually is. Grief is a response to a loss in our lives that feels irreplaceable. People have a horrible tendency to look at that loss and then judge whether or not it warrants sadness. It's easy to feel like our circumstances don't warrant the word *grief*. We tell ourselves that our situation isn't bad enough to feel grief. Someone else has it worse. But, frankly, that's absolute nonsense. We most often think of the loss of a person, but this could also be the loss of a job, a dream, a relationship, a friendship, a way of life, or even a vision we had for our lives. Only you can say if your loss is irreplaceable or not. If that is what you are feeling, let your heart grieve.

*Even in laughter the
heart may ache,
and rejoicing may
end in grief.*

Proverbs 14:13

No two people experience grief in exactly the same way. You may want to stay in bed for a week and cry, but your best friend may get angry and want to break things. No matter what we have lost or how we experience grief in our lives, we have to lean into it. If, instead, we choose to bury it or run away from it, we are telling ourselves that our pain doesn't matter, that it is unimportant compared to everything else we have going on. Which is simply untrue, not to mention that if we do that we are undermining our own experiences. Doesn't the world do that to us enough already? It's a choice to believe the lies that our grief doesn't matter or our pain isn't worthy of being dealt with. I hope you chose to believe the truth and let yourself grieve when you need to.

RINGS OF COMFORT

Have you heard of ring theory for how to handle grief? It was developed by psychologists Susan Silk and Barry Goldman. Here are the basics:

- Draw a circle. Write the names of the people dealing with grief in the middle of the circle. These should be the people most directly affected by the crisis or loss.

❧ Now draw a larger circle around the first circle. In this ring, write the names of the people who are next closest to the loss.

❧ Draw a larger circle and write the names of the people who are the next closest to the loss after the names in the second circle. Keep drawing circles until you run out of names. Now you have a comforting order.

❧ The person in the center of the circles can talk to anyone she wants to. She can complain and cry and grieve openly. Everyone else can also do these things, but, and *this is the key*, only to people in the rings outside of theirs.

❧ When you are talking to someone in a ring that is smaller than yours, your goal should be to comfort, support, encourage, and help. That means no complaining of your own, no giving advice, no sharing your own stories, and definitely no telling them to "get over it."

❧ When you are talking to someone in a larger ring than yours, feel free to share your feelings, cry, whine, or rage over how unfair the whole situation is. The rule is to give comfort in and dump your own feelings out.

This is helpful when you aren't sure what to do or say for a friend or loved one who is grieving. It's so natural to want to dish out advice or fix the situation or connect over a time that you also grieved, but that really isn't helpful. Keeping your ring position in mind can help make sure that you are there for your friend in a meaningful way that will make her feel supported and loved.

Before my breakdown in the car, I hadn't cried about our story in a while. I had become an expert at pretending I was okay. I wrote a lot on social media about my feelings because that was therapeutic for me, but I rarely cried about it. Instead I put on a brave face, pulled myself together, and filled my life with busyness to avoid dealing with the mess. It's not that I hate crying. But allowing myself to grieve goes against the very fiber of how I am wired. I am an Enneagram 2, the helper. I take care of the people in my life, no matter what. But my grief didn't care about any of that. It made me vulnerable. It took away my ability to pretend I was okay. It forced me to open myself up to the grace of letting my people help take care of me.

We are called to do life in community. But sometimes it can be so tough to let other people in, huh? I have been burned in the past by friends who should have been there for me and weren't. I wanted them to roll up their sleeves and walk through the hard stuff with me, and instead they ran. Ouch, right? Then there's the judgement from people who don't understand what you're feeling, those who tell you to "just get over it." Or the awkwardness from people who don't know what to say, so they avoid you.

I was so tired of opening up just to be told how I should or shouldn't be feeling by someone who had never walked this road that I stopped letting those closest to me in, even Blake. And Blake was walking right beside me. But building a wall around my heart to keep more pain away also kept love and support and encouragement and empathy away, and I desperately needed all of those things. Galatians 6:2 says, "Carry each other's burdens, and in this way you will fulfill the law of Christ." God has always known that we need each other. We need support and the perspective of others. When you are in the thick of the tough stuff, it's hard to see the whole picture. Having community around you can help you see past the details and on to the bigger picture. Wherever you find your community—at your church, your school, a club or organization, or a close-knit group of friends—don't shut them out when grief comes knocking. I promise that you will weather the storm better with them by your side.

The Bible is pretty clear on grief. Look at the story of Lazarus in John 11. You'll see that even though Jesus knew what would happen in the coming moments, He still wept over

"Blessed are those who mourn, for they will be comforted.

Matthew 5:4

the death of His friend. Did you know that the shortest verse in the entire Bible states, "Jesus wept?" So simple, yet so profound. Jesus knew that He would soon bring His friend back to life. But, even knowing that, He still grieved. This is powerful because Jesus is showing us how important grieving is in the healing process. If Jesus prioritized taking the time to grieve, then so can we.

RIDE THE WAVES

There will be days during a challenging season when I feel okay. But other days the grief crashes over me like a tidal wave, sucking me under and leaving me gasping for breath. No matter where I am at that moment or what I'm doing, I have learned that I have to stop and lean into that grief. After all, it's kinda tough to fight a wave. Better to let it wash over you and then get up and head back to dry land. Here are some ways I ride out a grief wave:

- write in my journal

- talk to a friend

- read an inspiring book or a comforting, old favorite

- watch a favorite movie or TV show

- take a walk in nature

- pray

- read my Bible

- listen to worship music

I try not to rush the process. I talk to God and tell Him honestly how I'm feeling. And then when I feel like the waves have passed, I take a deep breath, get myself together, and get up. As important as it is to lean into grief, we also have to keep getting back up.

"Do you feel like you are over it?"

This is a real question I have been asked, and let me tell you: receiving this question is excruciating. The thing about grief is that you are *never* over it. You don't move on from grief—you move forward *with* it. My heart bears the scars of every loss I have experienced. Yes, time, prayer, and community all help you heal, but even healed hurts leave scars. We have to learn how to move forward with our lives, continually making space for the pain that is now a part of us and our story. Grief and loss change us. Grief gives us a deeper level of empathy for what others are walking through. It opens our eyes to the pain in this world. It puts all of life in perspective and shifts our focus to what actually matters. Slowly and surely, brick by brick, God can build beauty out of the ashes, if you let Him. One choice at a time.

Stop and Reflect

What gifts has your grief given you?

_____

_____

_____

_____

_____

How have your difficult experiences given you a greater understanding of the world, of God, and of yourself?

_____

_____

_____

_____

What wisdom have you gained, and how can you share this with others so that they can learn to heal too?

_____

_____

_____

_____

_____

_____

_____

_____

_____

_____

_____

The greatest gift that came from my grief is empathy. Before infertility, I hadn't lost much in life. I didn't understand the depth of what others were walking through as they experienced sadness. I didn't understand why they couldn't move on. I still won't understand exactly what others experience or exactly how they feel because our stories are different. And you may feel that way about my story. You may not have walked this road, but you understand what it means to grieve and feel pain. And so do I. Because we know, we can empathize with others' pain and experiences instead of diminishing or discounting them.

Jesus was comfortable with the uncomfortable. He didn't hesitate to sit with people in their grief. If we want to be more like Him, we need to remember that and focus on becoming expert listeners and empathizers. And over and over again, we must remind one another that though the sadness may be different, we do not have to walk through it alone. We can keep going—together. As for me, moving forward with grief looks like continuing to live my life. It looks like choosing each day to be fully present. It looks like continuing to get back up every time the waves knock me down. It looks like taking the time I need to let my heart heal. It looks like taking the next step over and over again. And through the process of putting one foot in front of the other, I become stronger. I become more capable of handling and living through hard things. I become braver and less afraid of loss. And so do you.

I am the mother I am today because of my grief. I enjoy my kids on a deeper level than I might have because of the struggle I went through to have them. I have more patience and gratefulness in the moments that test me because of the sadness. I have not moved on. Those moments of loss and grief in my life still matter. They still shape me. They have made me who I am. I pray that I never forget the pain and instead use it to always create a more beautiful life.

Let's Pray

Heavenly Father,

Thank You for being with me as I grieve. It is so comforting to know that I am never alone with these heartbreaking feelings and that You understand perfectly how I'm feeling and grieve with me. Please help me to be brave enough to open up to my community about what I'm going through.

In Jesus's name, amen.

SEVEN

An attitude of grace

—

My dad officiated my wedding. I vividly remember him sharing a story about an older couple who had lots of disagreements. He used the story as an illustration that there would be days when Blake and I didn't see eye to eye. He explained that storms would come our way, and he challenged us to make a habit of getting on our knees together to pray because that's the best way to see eye to eye. As a smitten young couple, we couldn't even imagine storms. All we could see were clear skies and sunny days.

We started our married life in Blake's hometown in North Alabama, both working extremely low-paying jobs, but looking for better opportunities. That summer, I received an incredible job offer to work in pharmaceutical sales. The job required us to move to Auburn, a town we both loved. Blake and I weighed our options and decided to go for it. So, we put our house on the market, moved most of our stuff to storage, and started a new adventure in a tiny apartment in Auburn while we waited for our house to sell. We loved life in Auburn, but there was one small problem. By the time I accepted the job, it was too late in the summer for Blake to find a teaching job.

We spent the next year of our marriage supporting our-selves on my income plus any substitute teaching jobs Blake could get. It was hard for him to work odd jobs after leaving a job that he truly loved. As excited as we were about our new home, we had no idea how dark and hard the next year would be. Our house sat on the market for nine months before it sold. We watched the savings account we had worked so hard to build slowly and surely whittle away to nothing. To say we were stressed would be putting it mildly.

I wish I could say that we remembered my dad's wedding day advice and proactively treated each other with grace and empathy and kindness. But, instead, we let bitterness enter our marriage. It started out small but built nasty homes in our hearts over that year. Blake's bitterness grew because he'd left a job he loved, even though he truly believed the move was for the best. He hated not being able to contrib-ute much to our income. Meanwhile, the stress of being the family breadwinner in a brand-new job got to me. I needed to put in the time to really learn, and when I'd come home, exhausted, and Blake asked me about dinner plans or left his laundry piled up when he'd had the whole day off, it left me feeling resentful and angry. Little by little, bitterness sunk its roots deep into our hearts. In the spring of that year, Blake started looking for teaching jobs, which became a source of many, many fights for us because I didn't think

Be kind and compassionate to one another, forgiving each other, just as in Christ God forgave you.

Ephesians 4:32

he was doing it right or trying hard enough, and he wanted the space to do it his way.

I remember sitting in my car outside a doctor's office in a random town in Georgia, needing to go in for a sales call. Instead, I sat there for way too long sobbing because Blake and I had just a fight that felt marriage-shattering. We could not get on the same page no matter how many times we talked. I resented him for things I'd never shared. He resented me for things he'd never shared. We needed help. We could have given up right then, but instead we sought counseling. We learned that we hadn't been communicating well. We'd both been trying so hard to change each other that we had stopped really *seeing* each other. Instead of leaning in with grace and loving each other through these challenges, we'd almost let those challenges steal our love altogether. Boy, was that a wake-up call!

The battle to keep bitterness out of our hearts is something that most women fight their entire lives. Bitterness is like a splinter. It looks so tiny, but it can wreak incredible havoc if we don't remove it from our hearts and use grace to put boundaries in place to keep it out.

One of the biggest lies that leads to bitterness is that life should be fair. I don't know about you, but when I was a kid, my mom made sure that everything was equal at our house. If I got 6 chips, so did my brother and sisters. If my brother got a curfew of 11:00, I expected to be able to stay out that late too.

All that certainly kept us from squabbling, but it didn't exactly drive home the lesson we needed to learn, which is that life is inherently unfair. No two people's lives look exactly the same. But if we take our eyes off of our own story and look at others' around us, we may begin to think that we've gotten a raw deal or that we are somehow better than someone else because our story has been easier than theirs.

Have you compared or are you comparing your family to someone else's family? Or have you compared or are you comparing yourself to someone else's job or talents?

_____

_____

_____

_____

_____

Are you allowing these comparisons to make you feel less than or diminished or not good enough?

_____

_____

_____

_____

_____

Is a seed of bitterness growing in your heart because of it?

_____

_____

_____

_____

_____

_____

_____

_____

During that first year of marriage, it seemed like all of our friends were living easy lives with perfect jobs and no financial stress. I know you've heard the saying that comparison is the thief of joy, but really comparison is a one-way ticket for bitterness to claim space in our hearts. When we compare ourselves to others, we quickly become discontent with what we have.

We all have different gifts, different struggles, different joys, different careers, different financial stats, and different stories. And that's exactly what makes life and the body of Christ beautiful because we all bring something different—and unique—to the table. It's not the seeing of what others have that causes problems, it's the envy of what they have that leads us down a path of bitterness.

Tell me if this sounds familiar. You're relaxing on the couch and you start scrolling through social media when you stop on

There are different kinds
of gifts... there are different
kinds of service... There are
different kinds of working,
but in all of them and in everyone
it is the same God at work.

1 Corinthians 12:4–6

the account of someone using her gifts in an amazing way. You click over to her feed and lose yourself in her beautiful pictures and inspiring captions and you think, *Gosh I wish I was doing that.* Or maybe you scroll and see a friend's magazine-worthy family picture and think, *Wow, I wish our family was perfect like that.* Or maybe you see announcement posts of the big news *you've* been hoping for, and it makes you feel less than or mad that it's not you. Isn't that just the worst feeling?

I know you've heard this before, but let me tell you again: the grass is rarely ever greener. Everyone has her burdens to carry and her crosses to bear whether they are plain to see or not. We're only seeing one snapshot of someone's life or one message about her success. We rarely get to see the messy, heartbreaking parts, so we compare one moment of her life to our messy reality, and suddenly bitterness blooms.

Another lie that's easy to get sucked into is that life is perfect for everyone else. I think it's gotten way worse with social media because we fill our minds and our hearts with everyone else's highlight reel. Most people don't share their mess on the Internet. And I don't blame them. Do you? But still we choose to continually, day after day, spend time scrolling. As you mindlessly scroll, you know that what you're seeing isn't a true representation of anyone's life, but somehow you turn down that voice of truth. Subconsciously, we start believing the lie, and the door for bitterness opens.

DIGITAL GRACE

If this chapter is resonating with you, then I want to challenge you to take a digital time out. That means no social media, no blogs, no news sites, and no online shopping. Try it for a week, but even a break for a day or two can help your heart immensely.

Instead of mindlessly scrolling and liking, filling up and abandoning online shopping carts, and comparing our homes and closets to bloggers' refreshed living rooms and OOTDs, take the time to do something that actually makes you feel good. You'll be shocked at the amount of time you have! Go to that challenging barre class, cook yourself your favorite meal from scratch, take a bubble bath and listen to your favorite music, check out a new book from the library and get lost in it, or go for a hike with your bestie.

Remind yourself what it feels like to *live* your life instead of documenting it. Once your break is over, try to limit your online time. We set screen limits for our kiddos, so why not for ourselves? If it's not good for them, it's not good for us either!

Scrolling is addictive; our curiosity drives us to see more, know more, learn more. The creators of apps intentionally structure them to keep us coming back for more. They want to be successful, and who can blame them? I am not saying social media is a bad thing. There is so much good that comes from those spaces on the Internet. But we have to keep it in its rightful place and recognize the impact, intentionally or unintentionally, that it's making on our hearts.

So let's pour a little grace into our online lives. That means making sure your online world is one that inspires you, challenges you, and uplifts you. Is one account continually triggering thoughts of jealousy? Unfollow her. Not because she's bad, but because it's what is right and best for *your* heart. Grace for our online selves is recognizing what or who triggers the discontentment in our hearts and putting up boundaries, even if that means taking a social media break or going on an unfollow spree. When we set unrealistic and unattainable standards for ourselves, we will stay in a state of discontentment, allowing bitterness to fester and grow.

Stop and Reflect

Is there someone in your life who somehow always leaves you feeling jealous?

_____

_____

_____

_____

_____

_____

_____

_____

_____

_____

_____

_____

What do you think it is about her that draws you into the comparison trap?

_____

_____

_____

_____

_____

_____

_____

_____

_____

_____

_____

_____

What work can you do for yourself or your circumstances to address that issue?

_____

_____

_____

_____

_____

_____

_____

_____

_____

_____

I wish I could say that Blake and I learned our lesson about letting bitterness into our marriage, but nothing could have prepared us for the marathon that is caring for newborn twins. We had five years together as just us before the boys arrived, and we had made it through the ups and downs of IVF as a unified team, so I was overly confident that we would have no issues parenting. But when you have a hormonal, sleep-deprived new mother in close quarters with an overworked, overtired father plus two babies, well, that's a recipe for disaster.

I have to admit that in the first year of our boys' lives, bitterness not only set up a home in my heart, but I am pretty sure it built a whole village in there. And it was all directed toward Blake. I remember deliriously scrolling through social media seeing all of these smiling, happy pictures and romantic gestures by other new dads, and it made me so jealous. Nothing Blake did was good enough. He didn't walk into the house happy enough. He didn't smile when I asked him for help changing diapers. (I mean, c'mon! Who does smile at the thought of changing a stinky one?) He didn't offer to help me fast enough. I was holding him to ridiculous standards because I was comparing his actions to a few photos on Instagram about other dads.

Once I got a little caught up on sleep and communicated how I was feeling, I realized I was being ridiculous and terribly unfair to Blake. He's a man of few words and literally no one ever would describe him as a romantic. But he shows his love through faithful acts of service, daily check-ins and "I love yous," and being a committed partner to me who values my input and opinions. We will never have an Instagram marriage with emotional comments to each other, grand gestures to be used as content, or romantic, staged photos and stories, and I will gladly take our healthy, real marriage any day of the week! But I had to refocus my heart and mind to recognize and appreciate what made Blake special and our marriage work. As I remembered, recognized, and began to cherish the things I loved most about Blake, the bitterness faded quickly.

Banish Relationship Bitterness

When I feel bitterness and resentment creeping into my heart towards Blake (or a friend or family member), I know it's time to cover that person in grace and love. Here's how I do it:

- Identify the source of the bitterness. Is it really something he's done, or are my friend's stories about things her husband does making me jealous?

- Look at how I'm treating him. Is something I'm doing (or not doing) likely to cause resentment? If I'm feeling resentful, he probably is as well.

- Write out what's bothering me and then clearly communicate it to him so I can erase my mental scoreboard and we can get on the same page.

- Make a list of all the ways that he gives me grace and love.

- Make a list of everything I love about him.

- Write him a letter or card expressing how much I love

him and why, and sneak it into his car or bag for a surprise.

≫ Do something kind for him without expecting anything in return.

In marriage and in life, it's so important to focus our time and energy on watering our own grass. If someone else's grass looks greener, it might be simply because they are watering and caring for it consistently. One of the ways that Blake and I do this in our marriage is to take time away from the kids to observe each other in our element.

I knew I wanted to marry Blake when I went to watch him during his student teaching. Watching him pour his heart out for those kids, I knew he'd be the best dad. And he is. So, even now, my favorite thing to do is to go watch Blake coach his basketball team. Watching him in his element doing what he was created to do ignites my love for him all over again. It reminds me that the work he is doing outside of our home matters so much.

Water the grass you are standing on with grace. Pluck the weeds. Mow faithfully. Meticulously trim the edges so there is room for love and gratitude to grow. Be faithful where God has you. Whatever is causing the seeds of discontentment and bitterness to bloom in your heart, root it out so that you can spend time making your own grass extra green.

Let's Pray

Heavenly Father,

Please help me to replace any bitterness, jealousy, or resentment in my heart with grace and love. I'm so grateful for all the beautiful blessings You have given me. Sometimes, I get distracted and start comparing my life to others, but I don't want to! Please help me to be mindful of this tendency and stop it in its tracks when it happens. Instead, I want to focus on all the blessings in my life and taking good care of them and my people.

In Jesus' name, amen.

EIGHT

*The grace
of faith*

—

I grew up in a family of believers. My dad is a pastor, so, for as long as I can remember, we learned about Jesus at home, at school, and at church. I attended a private Christian school from pre-K through senior year, including daily Bible class and weekly chapel. I know all the Bible stories, the well-known and the lesser so. I know the Christmas story by heart. At age seven, I gave my life to the Lord. My faith has always been a part of my life, but it was not my own in those early days. I didn't realize it until much later, but I was living on borrowed faith from my parents, my teachers, and my mentors. I took it all for granted because I had been spoon-fed the gospel my whole life.

In high school, my heart grew numb to all things Christian. I don't have a dramatic testimony or some harrowing story, but I did rebel and test all the boundaries. I drank alcohol illegally. I lied. I got my bellybutton pierced because I knew my parents would hate it. I went way too far with my high school boyfriend. I said I was a believer, but I wasn't really acting like one.

The summer before my senior year of high school, my

parents made me volunteer at a Christian summer camp called Kanakuk. I was dreading it and furious at my parents for making me work all summer for free. My job there was to work as a nanny for one of the staff families alongside a girl named Sarah. There was no way I could have anticipated how much Sarah would inspire me and change my life.

That summer I watched Sarah pursue Jesus from a front-row seat, not because she had to but because she *wanted* to. I saw her make mistakes, own up to them, and ask for forgiveness. I saw her receive grace firsthand when she messed up and I saw her give grace so freely to everyone around her. For the first time in my life, I witnessed the freedom that comes from walking with God. Back home, living the life of a believer felt more like a set of rules that had to be followed. It all felt outdated and legalistic, and most of those rules seemed to be more about judgement and shame then love and joy. But Sarah showed me that following Jesus was a journey of grace and truth and mercy and freedom.

For the first time, I wanted faith. I wanted what she had. I wanted Jesus. During that summer, my faith began to become my own. I was able to ask questions without fear of judgement and lean on someone like Sarah to show me the way. I admired her authenticity, her caring heart, her willingness to be real and vulnerable with me. She never pretended to have it all together. And I loved that. I could relate to it. That summer changed me.

The God of all grace,
who called you to his
eternal glory in Christ,
after you have suffered a
little while, will himself
restore you and make you
strong, firm and steadfast.

1 Peter 5:10

Jesus changed me through a girl named Sarah who was simply showing up to do her job alongside me.

Through that season of searching, I learned that you can say you believe something as much as you want, but that doesn't make it true. Actions, not words, are a more honest look at what a person believes. I knew what the Bible said, and I believed it to be true. But I had no idea *why*. Did I believe just because my parents did? Or because that's how I was raised?

As my personal relationship with Jesus deepened, I spent a lot of time in the Word to find the answers to questions that mattered to me. How do my actions reflect what I believe? How do I stand up to temptation? How do I face hard things? How do I react when I am left with unmet desires? Do I rise up against the darkness, or am I overcome by it? How do I act when no one is looking?

You've heard the saying "If you don't stand for something, you'll fall for anything." There's a lot of truth in that. I have always admired the bravery of those I've watched take a stand, and I wanted to take bold stands for what I believed in. I wanted my life to have purpose. I wanted to make waves for the kingdom. But you cannot stand up for what you believe if you don't know *why* you believe. You cannot share the radical grace of Jesus with others if you don't understand it yourself. You have to have a firm foundation to build on.

Stop and Reflect

How do my actions reflect what I believe?

_____

_____

_____

_____

_____

_____

_____

_____

How do I stand up to temptation?

_____

_____

_____

_____

_____

_____

_____

_____

How do I face hard things?

_____

_____

_____

_____

_____

_____

_____

_____

_____

_____

How do I react when I am left with unmet desires?

_____

_____

_____

_____

_____

_____

_____

_____

_____

Do I rise up against the darkness, or am I overcome by it?

_____

_____

_____

_____

_____

_____

_____

_____

_____

How do I act when no one is looking?

_____

_____

_____

_____

_____

_____

_____

_____

_____

I spent my college years figuring out why I wanted to follow Jesus, why I claimed to be a Christian, and why my faith mattered to me. I did the work to grow spiritually. I found a

Since we have been
justified through faith,
we have peace with
God through our
Lord Jesus Christ.

Romans 5:1

church and I joined a Bible study. I surrounded myself with solid Christian friends. I had mentors pouring in, and I had accountability in my life. During these years my faith grew. As I learned about who God is and what His Word says with a heart that was willing to receive it, I gained more and more confidence to stand in faith as temptations came and difficulties happened to me and to those around me. For the first time, my faith became my own. I felt so much more confident in letting go and trusting God because I truly believed what He said. I believed He would fulfill His promises and give me the strength to face anything that came my way.

For most of my life, I was surrounded by Christians. I never questioned the Bible stories I'd heard over and over again. But after college, I made a new friend named Kara, who had recently become a Christian. She did not grow up in church, so she was reading the Bible for the first time. Seeing the Bible through her eyes was like seeing it for the first time again.

One night Kara called me, and immediately after I said hello, she asked, "Do you really believe that Jonah was swallowed by a whale? Like a whale ate him? And what about Noah? He legit built a giant boat, and God killed everyone else on the earth? Do you believe these things actually happened or are they just stories to make a point?"

I honestly didn't know what to say at first. No one had ever asked me those questions, and I'd never asked those questions myself. After some thought I told her that I believed that the Bible is God's Word, and it is true. Every word of it. And because I believe that, I had to choose to believe everything that's in it. If I decided to pick apart the Bible and accept the Word as also having non-truths, then why would I believe *any* of it? It is either God's Word or it's not. It's either true or it's not. In its entirety. It's an all-or-nothing thing.

That experience with Kara was the first time I had to stand up for what I believed in. Not in a defending-my-faith kind of way, but more of a sharing-the-gospel kind of way. She was searching honestly for the truth, and I had the privilege of helping guide her on her journey. She didn't want me to simply tell her that I believed, but she wanted to hear why. Specifically, how had I personally seen God work in my life? How did I know it was God? Kara challenged me with her questions, and to be honest, I didn't have all the answers. But I was determined to find the answers because it mattered. How could I stand up for what I believed in if I couldn't verbalize why I believed?

Have you ever been challenged like that? I was lucky that Kara was asking because she genuinely wanted to understand, not to be antagonistic. It can be really frustrating when someone challenges your beliefs or faith just to cause drama. Hello comments sections on the Internet! You can tell pretty quickly who is genuinely interested in learning and discussing and who is only trying to make you feel or look ignorant. Conversations

Consider it pure joy,
my brothers and
sisters, whenever you
face trials of many
kinds, because you
know that the
testing of your faith
produces perseverance.

James 1:2–3

with the genuinely interested are always worth having. These conversations will push you, challenge you, and make you think. Of course, you won't ever have all the answers, which is why it's important to surround yourself with like-minded friends and mentors who can encourage you and help you figure out what you don't know yet. But it's also important to step outside your safe zone and extend a hand to people who are searching. This is how we grow and ultimately learn how our faith gives us the strength to stand strong for what we believe.

Shore Up Your Foundation

Check out these excellent books that explain the *why* behind what we believe as Christians.

- *The Case for Christ* by Lee Strobel

- *The Complete Bible Answer Book* by Hank Hanegraff

- *God's Not Dead* by Rice Broocks

- *Evidence That Demands a Verdict* by Josh McDowell and Sean McDowell, PhD

🌿 *A Shot of Faith (to the Head)* by Mitch Stokes, PhD

🌿 *How to Talk About Jesus (Without Being That Guy)* by Sam Chan

🌿 *Seeking Allah, Finding Jesus* by Nabeel Qureshi

Trusting is what we do when we believe God. It's an exercise of our faith. Because we believe, we trust. Because we know Him, we trust. Because we've seen what He's done in our lives and in the lives of others, we trust. We have confidence in who He is and what He says He's going to do. We have a peace that comes from knowing He will be with us, even when our circumstances feel unsettling. Trusting is taking the step even when we cannot see the road ahead. It's flying blind, but securely, because we know He's guiding the way.

Trusting means releasing our fears. And we all have fears, both big and small. Having fears doesn't make us unbelievers; it makes us human. A huge step in trusting God is acknowledging the fear that is holding you back. Call it out. And then take the step anyway, knowing God will cover you in His grace. Trust is having confidence in God, despite your fear.

This type of faith and trust is not developed overnight. It's developed after walking through some stuff—some *hard* stuff. With each storm that I made it through, both my faith and trust grew. As your faith grows, you learn you can trust Jesus a little bit more. My faith and trust in God grow exponentially each time I look back and take note of all that He has brought me through, when I see all the ways He's been faithful in my life.

Don't run from the hard stuff. You might be in a difficult, maybe even heartbreaking, season right now. I bet there's some stuff you wish wasn't a part of your story. Don't run from it. There is purpose in it beyond what you can see. God has the master plan, and He can see what you can't yet. He will use you through this if you let Him.

Let's Pray

Father God,

I want my faith in You to be as firm as it can be. Please direct my reading to help deepen my understanding of You and Your calling for me. Thank You for Your grace as I ask questions and make mistakes and search for the answers. I know I will only see partly for now and look forward to the day I will see fully with You.

In Christ's name, amen.

NINE

The grace of hope

———

When I was pregnant with the twins, Blake and I talked a lot about ideal timing for a third baby. We wanted to try again after the boys were two so that they would be almost three when the baby was born. As we got closer and closer to the date we said we'd try again, part of me felt ready and part of me felt like I was still drowning in the chaos of twin life. I'd never felt so busy and scattered before in my entire life. We were just entering the "terrible twos" and beginning the exhausting stage of discipline. Ready or not, we decided to transfer our sixth embryo that fall.

It failed. I was blindsided by the news. I knew in the back of my mind that it *could* fail, but I was so sure that it wouldn't. Going into the procedure, I felt so confident. And then the call came. Not pregnant. Even as I held my two miracles in my arms, my heart broke all over again. It sent me back to where I'd been three years earlier, and all the familiar grief came flooding back into my heart.

I was tired of crying over my story, but I also knew that I needed to grieve this loss. So there I sat, crying over yet another failed attempt to bring life into this world, another precious baby lost to us forever. This transfer cost us $10,000. I had poured so much medicine into my body. I had missed time with my boys and my business to prepare. And the worst part? I knew now in a way that I hadn't fully known before exactly what I was missing out on. I looked my boys in the eyes, and I grieved over the loss of the life that could have been with that little embryo. I pictured birthday parties and middle-of-the-night feedings and first steps and those chubby little hands holding mine and I wept.

Over the next few months, my heart grew numb. I didn't feel sad. I didn't feel frustrated. I didn't feel *anything*. As we navigated all the decisions about when to try again, I was simply going through the motions. I was unintentionally building walls around my heart because I was so sick of experiencing the same heartbreak. I was tired of riding the roller coaster of emotion.

As Blake and I discussed our options, we realized that we had felt optimistic the transfer would work simply because our last transfer had worked. But, the last time, with the transfer that led to the twins, we had prayed heaven down. We had rallied our prayer warriors. We had prayed, we had fasted, and we had begged God to breathe life into those embryos like our lives depended on it. We didn't just have hope. We *chose* hope. We *lived* hope. We focused our eyes on Jesus, the One who *is* hope, and ran toward Him with everything we had. We did none of those things this time around. Yes, we prayed. But nothing like we had before. And that had everything to do with why my heart was so numb.

Why, my soul,
are you downcast?
Why so disturbed
within me?
Put your hope in
God, for I will yet
praise him,
my Savior and
my God.

Psalm 42:5

I had allowed my desire to become my hope. I think we often confuse the two when, in reality, they are very different. Desire is what a person wants. But a desire's strength is inconsistent; it rises and falls with human emotion. Biblical hope is the confident trust that God will fulfill His promises. Biblical hope is steeped in grace. The strength of biblical hope rests on the faithfulness of God Himself. Through His grace, we are blessed with miracles whether we deserve them or not. Doesn't that just give you chills in the best way? None of us are owed a thing by God, but He pours His grace out to us anyway, blessing richly and fully. How lucky are we?

Still, despite knowing all of that, we continually place our hope in all the wrong things. Even the best of things—doctors, jobs, relationships, our kids, love—aren't God. And when we place our hope in temporary things that can never completely or indefinitely satisfy, we will always be disappointed.

Stop and Reflect

Is there something you are desperately hoping for right now?

_____

_____

_____

_____

Is your hope for that centered in Jesus? Or is your hope placed somewhere else?

_____

_____

_____

_____

How can you shift that hope to center it in God?

_____

_____

_____

_____

The sad part of this story is that I knew better. I knew where my hope should be. I knew that hoping in the wrong places led to heartbreak. But I got lazy. And I got busy. I allowed the busyness of raising my boys, being a coach's wife, and running a business to be an excuse not to be faithful in my walk with the Lord. My quiet times rarely happened, but I had all the excuses, of course. And when I did spend time with God, those times were filled with so much distraction.

Once again, I was living on borrowed faith. I was using the best doctor at the best clinic, and our embryo had a good quality score. Check, check, check. I checked the boxes off in my head and mapped out the plan for how it all would go. *My* plan. Not *His* plan. I wanted to have a third baby around the time when the boys would turn three. I liked that age gap. I wanted to deliver in early summer, so Blake would be home more to help me. We made all these decisions around what worked best *for us* without even asking God what He wanted for our story. We took back the reins and were writing the story of how we wanted it to go. Our hope was not in Jesus. Our misplaced hope was staked firmly in *our* plan.

So afterward, then the transfer failed and I wrestled over my numb heart, I began to pray and cry out to God. Why this same heartbreak again? I'll never forget the moment when I stared at my miracle twins, and I felt this truth so clearly placed on my heart. I couldn't stop thinking, *They were not my plan.* Over and over that phrase went through my head.

My plan was to have our first baby seven years ago. My plan was not IVF. My plan was to get pregnant the first time we tried. *They were not my plan.* They were *His* plan. Every part of my boys' lives was not my plan. I never wanted twins. I didn't want to give birth in August as Blake and my mom started back to school. God's plan was hard. But as I sat there on that couch snuggled up to the cutest miracles I've ever seen, none of that hard stuff felt heavy anymore. Why? Because God got me through it all. As I hugged my babies and tears fell down my face, the fog lifted and took the numbness with it.

We wait in hope
for the LORD;
he is our help
and our shield.

Psalm 33:20

In that quiet and sweet, still moment, God reminded me in the most gentle way that these tiny little faces I get to look at every single day were never part of *my* plan. But they were always part of His plan. If I had to do it all again, I'd choose His plan every time. How had I forgotten this? I beat myself up over this for a while. But no matter how long you've been walking with God, you can get distracted and forget the lessons you worked so hard to learn. When you aren't faithful in the little things, your heart becomes more susceptible to the lies, and you start placing your hope in things that will never satisfy.

I cannot place my hope in my plans. I must seek Him, walk with Him, trust Him, and allow Him to direct my path. I have to place my hopes in the One who never disappoints and is the same yesterday, today, and tomorrow. Luckily, God's grace has us covered. He will patiently, kindly, and gently teach us the same lessons over and over again until they are written on our hearts.

Hope is a choice. It is both a noun and a verb. It's something you can have, but also something you can do. To me the more important of the two is always in the doing. If we have hope, but aren't actively hoping, then we are missing a crucial component. The hoping is God's grace in action in our life. It's that confident trust we place in Him to bless us regardless of the circumstances, the difficulties, or the downright impossibilities.

Guide me in your truth and teach me, for you are God my Savior, and my hope is in you all day long.

Psalm 25:5

HOPE IN HOPELESS TIMES

So how do you cling to hope when your circumstances feel hopeless? You surround yourself with people who share your hope. Keep the hopeful people close and the negative people at a distance. Give yourself grace from the guilt of distancing yourself from anyone who steals your hope. You can still love people from afar. Give people the grace to be where they are in their lives, but be intentional about putting space where it's best for *your* heart.

Do not give up. As you pursue the desires of your heart and the assignments God calls you to, you must constantly evaluate what is working and what is not. Make adjustments, be flexible, and hold tight to your hope, but hold your desires loosely. We all know that God's answer to that desire could still be no. But if it's no, it's because He has a better desire for you, a better plan that you just can't see yet. That is the hope to hold onto. The idea is not to keep trying again and again until you get what you want. It's to keep getting back up each time you face heartbreak because God is not done with you yet. He has called you to this day, this time, this moment. His plan is the one to keep hoping for, so don't give up. He's worth it.

Have you ever heard the phrase "Don't get your hopes up?" That phrase is an insurance policy based in fear, a reminder to ourselves to set our expectations low so that failure won't hurt so badly. I hate the lack of grace in that expression. If our hopes are in Jesus, they can never be too high. I want to choose hope over fear. Fear that I won't get the thing I desire. Fear that this season will never end. Fear that I am going to fail. Fear of what others may think about me. Instead of allowing those fears to dictate our steps, let's choose hope.

Choosing hope gives us something to look forward to. It strengthens our hearts when we stand and believe that God is able. Choosing hope is a way we actively live out our faith. Choosing hope means that we believe God's promises are true, that we believe His plan for our lives is good. Choosing hope means that we believe God will create beauty from ashes and purpose from the pain in our lives. Choosing hope means believing that even if God's answer is no, we will be okay.

Hope allows you to believe that God will work all things for our good and His purpose. It's so much more than just wishful thinking. Hope has the power to shift your attitude in the middle of sadness because hope tells you that, in Jesus, brighter days are ahead. He promises us in Psalm 30:5 that "weeping may stay for the night, but rejoicing comes in the morning."

Martin Luther King Jr. said, "We must accept finite disappointment but never lose infinite hope." No matter how many times you face sadness or how dark your circumstances feel, I encourage you to keep choosing hope. Start by getting up each day and trusting that today will be better than yesterday. Choose hope day by day, hour by hour, and sometimes minute by minute. I encourage you to keep practicing, keep choosing hope, give yourself grace when you stumble, and day by day your faith, trust, and hope will grow strong and bold.

Let's Pray

Dearest Lord,

Thank You for the gift of hope. I know that my hope is never misplaced in You. Please continue to teach me the hard lessons until I know the truth of them in my heart, my bones, and my soul. Thank You for giving me grace as I struggle to truly know Your truth.

In Your Son's name, amen.

TEN

Grace in gratitude

Stepping into motherhood after four draining years of infertility was strange. I had wanted to be a mom for an achingly long time, but I had a trouble wrapping my mind and heart around the reality that it was happening. My whole pregnancy felt surreal. The moment I had waited and prayed over for so long had almost arrived, but, even as I felt my boys move around in my womb and watched my stomach grow, the experience didn't feel real. Reality finally hit me when doctors placed two newborns on my chest.

I'd heard people talk about that moment so many times. I'd played it out in my head often as I anticipated their birth. Women shared how special and magical birth was, and I'd read over and over that moms looked into their babies' eyes, and it was love at first sight.

This was not my experience at all.

Did I love them instantly? Yes. But there was nothing magical about the moment. I was in a fog from all the pain medicine I'd been given during and after my C-section. I sat there in the recovery room in a bit of a daze and stared at these two strangers who'd lived inside of me for nine months.

I didn't know them at all. Who were they going to be? Would they be alike or different? Were they going to be easy or difficult babies, good or bad sleepers? Would they be shy and reserved or full of personality? I had so much to learn about my miracles.

Those first few days in the hospital were rough. Blake hadn't really held many babies before and had definitely never changed a diaper. I was mostly confined to a bed to give the incision from my C-section time to heal. I struggled to manage the pain and do simple things like move to the recliner or walk a lap around the hospital floor. The hospital wouldn't take the boys to the nursery, and they didn't allow family to stay the night. This meant Blake and I were on our own those first sleepless nights. Between Blake trying to figure out how to soothe our little guys, me juggling my recovery while also trying to figure out how to breastfeed two very different babies, I felt sure we were going to lose it. In the wee hours of the second morning, I texted my sister: SOS. *Please get here now. We need help. I don't even care how you have to sneak back here. Please find a way!!!*

During those first few days, fear crept in. Doubt crept in. A new level of exhaustion slapped on top. How would I recover from an intense surgery and care for two babies at one time? It was the beginning of football season, which meant taking extra time off was not an option for Blake. After the second

Because of the LORD's
great love we are not consumed,
for his compassions never fail.
They are new every morning;
great is your faithfulness.

Lamentations 3:22–23

day in the hospital, the staff helped us pack and sent us home with two newborns to keep alive. This was the beginning of the hardest year of our lives.

As a new mother, I'd never been more exhausted in my entire life. Stisher was my smaller baby, and he was a terrible eater. Every feed (which was every two to three hours at first) felt like a struggle. It took him way longer than normal to eat, which meant my already short breaks between feeds were even shorter. In the very early days, I basically spent all of my time nursing them, which meant that Blake and my mom were on burping, diapering, and soothing duty. It took Blake and me a while to find our groove. He'd try to soothe one and then give up and hand him to me. I'd do the same thing Blake tried, and the baby would calm down instantly. I can't tell you how many times Blake said to me, "I just did that!" He was trying really hard to help and often felt like it wasn't enough.

A few months before the boys were born, we shut down my business because I wanted and needed to be more present at home. But without my income, we were barely scraping by on Blake's teaching salary. And two babies means twice the expenses. Thankfully I was nursing and pumping to feed our boys because I don't think we even could have afforded formula at that point! My life had shifted from running an amazing company that produced beautiful and meaningful products with a fourteen-person staff to wiping rear ends, cleaning up vomit, pumping or nursing every hour and a half, and living in the same clothes for days at a time. Blake was working long hours that drained him, and then he came home to pure chaos with no chance to rest.

I already told you that bitterness crept in and that Blake and I were both short-tempered and not all that nice to each other. But that was only half of it. I'm not going to lie, I felt completely lost in the sea of motherhood. Like being a mama was completely taking over my entire identity. It was what I'd longed for, but that didn't make it easy. As much as I tried not to, I resented the fact that Blake left for work each day to do what he loved and have a break from the newborn insanity. His life had changed, of course, but not nearly as much as mine had. I needed a lifeline to remind me who I was outside of just a milk machine. I kept expecting Blake to give me that lifeline, but I wasn't communicating to him that I even needed it. I just didn't have the words for what I was experiencing.

These were the days—being blessed with children—that we had prayed so hard for, but they didn't feel like a blessing sometimes. They felt very far from what I imagined they'd be. As hard as that year was, the grace of God and my gratitude for the boys' lives carried me through. I had very little control, but the one thing I could control was my attitude. Attitude is a choice, and, after a few months, I realized that

So then, just as you received Christ Jesus as Lord, continue to live your lives in him, rooted and built up in him, strengthened in the faith as you were taught, and overflowing with thankfulness.

Colossians 2:6–7

I had been choosing bitterness and that needed to stop. Like yesterday.

I slowly, haltingly, started to choose gratitude. Sometimes I made that choice minute by minute, but eventually it got easier. On those dark days, I looked into my boys' faces, and my heart was filled with gratitude. They were God's plan, God's grace made flesh for me. He didn't promise me babies, but He gave them to me as a gift. A gift I didn't deserve, but would praise God for forever. When I was living in gratitude, I found that grace flowed so much more easily. I had more grace for Blake, more grace for Stisher and Elijah, and, probably most importantly, more grace for myself.

I desperately needed that grace. I needed to be so much kinder to myself as I figured out how to be a mom to my two little boys. I needed to forgive myself for my missteps and mistakes and my inability to "do it all." (Who came up with that nonsense anyway?) I had to give myself grace when exhaustion made it hard for me to think straight or get anything done. I needed to douse my expectations of motherhood in grace to wash away the unnecessary and unrealistic and keep only what truly mattered. I needed the grace to find my footing as my identity shifted and morphed with the waves of motherhood. I needed grace to combat the loneliness and uncertainty and doubt that had become my constant companions. I needed God's grace so much and, when I asked, He gave it freely.

Stop and Reflect

How can you choose gratitude over bitterness today?

_____

_____

_____

_____

_____

_____

_____

_____

_____

Is there somewhere in your life that you desperately need grace?

_____

_____

_____

_____

_____

_____

_____

_____

How can you give that grace to yourself? How can you ask God for more of the grace you need?

_____

_____

_____

_____

_____

_____

_____

_____

_____

_____

_____

We all have hard seasons, don't we? Sometimes it feels like being an adult is just one, long, difficult season punctuated with moments of joy. But no matter how dark or long or destructive a storm is, the sun always comes out again, bringing its own form of grace. The grace of light and warmth and flowers in bloom. The grace of green, growing things, and new life, and clear skies. Try to remember those sunny moments when you are standing in the storm. Hold on to that hope and grace and let it keep your attitude positive and your heart open to receive all of the blessings God has in store for you.

Jesus tells us John 16:33: "I have told you these things, so that in me you may have peace. In this world you will have trouble. But take heart! I have overcome the world." God is giving us the recipe for peace right here. The first part of the verse tells us that we will have trouble. It's a non-negotiable. A certifiable fact. There is no one who can escape having troubles. Yes, even that too-perfect influencer you follow who seems to be literally nonstop #blessed. You are not alone in struggling.

Then, God says to take heart. What does that mean? In a biblical sense, it means to be encouraged, to have hope, to be courageous, and not to give up. When we allow ourselves to take heart in Jesus, we receive His grace and actively put our hope in Him. Finally, He says, "I have overcome the world." Whoa. This is the very crux of God's grace for us. God overcame the world for you and me. We never could have overcome the world to make it to heaven on our own. Not a single one of us. So God made Jesus the living embodiment of His grace and sent Him to overcome for us. It's a done deal. That battle has already been won. Jesus is standing beside us through every trouble and every storm, holding His peace out to us like a gift. All we have to do is reach out and take it. What an incredible blessing this is!

This recipe for peace is how you shift your perspective about your situation. This truth is something you can keep going back to when the storms of life come your way. When you fill your heart with the peace that only God can provide, you become a wellspring of gratitude and grace. You can only give grace away once you have a heart *full* of it. And when your heart is full of grace, joy becomes your constant companion.

COUNT YOUR BLESSINGS

There are so many things in my daily life that I take for granted, even unintentionally so. Maybe you could say the same thing. When was the last time you thanked God for a roof over your head? Or meals every day, your health, or the luxury to buy a book? These are some of the simple things in life that I have taken for granted. Writing down the blessings in my life helps me recognize just how much I have to be thankful for, and once you start this practice, you might be surprised how suddenly your attitude shifts.

MY BLESSINGS

1.

2.

3.

4.

5.

6.

7.

8.

I'm not a big fan of the word *happy*. It feels circumstan-
tial. It feels temporary. And *happiness* is not a goal that God
directs us to in the Bible. But *joy* is a word I love. Joy is deeply
rooted in gratitude and grace. It's not easily taken away. It can
stand up to the storms of life. While happiness feels momen-
tary, joy feels lasting. We choose joy not out of obligation, but
as an act of worship. We choose joy because we know God

has already overcome the world. Being filled with joy doesn't mean that we can't be sad. We should feel sadness when we need to. We should allow ourselves to grieve. But deep and genuine joy gives us the strength to get up, take a step forward, and look around with gratitude at all the beautiful blessings in our lives.

So often we allow others' gifts or strengths or blessings to make us feel less than. My challenge to you is to change that. I want you to look for the joy inherent in what you have right this second. For example, instead of being envious that your friend just got a brand-new car, you can decide to be grateful and joyful that you have a working car. Instead of wishing you had her talent, thank God for the gifts He's given you that make you unique.

Maybe having kids was easy for you, but not for your friend. Or maybe you didn't have to study quite as hard to excel in college. There will always be things that others have that we don't; and there are also many blessings that we have that others are praying for. So rather than focusing on what you don't have or what you wish you had, be intentional about focusing on all the blessings you've had in the past, all you have now, and all God has waiting for you in the future. Let joy fill you so that you can recognize your blessings and be happy for the blessings of others. When we start to let in joy and peace, grace flows freely into our hearts and also from our hearts.

Let's Pray

Father God,

Thank You for the blessings You have heaped on me. Help me to continue to see them clearly. I want my heart to be filled with joy and peace because of all the good work You have done in my life.

In Your Son's name, amen.

ELEVEN

A community of grace

—

When we began our first IVF cycle, my best friend (we'll call her Becky) told me that she and her husband were going to try for a baby as well. I was filled with optimism that IVF would be the answer to our prayers and couldn't wait to talk through motherhood with Becky. I could just picture our kids becoming best friends too.

That June looked very different for us. My month was filled with shots, hormones, crazy mood swings, ultrasounds, blood work, and swelling from growing eggs. Becky's month was spent in bed with her husband as they embarked on this exciting journey ahead. We kept each other updated so we could pray specifically for each other's journeys. We promised each other that no matter what, we would both share the news when we found out. Good or bad, we wanted to walk through it together.

My news arrived first. As you've already read, it was a mess. Becky came over to see me when we got home that night. There was an unspoken awkwardness in the room because I didn't know if she had taken a test or not, but in my heart, I already knew. I knew she was pregnant. I had no actual evidence, but I felt God speaking to my spirit as He prepared me for the road ahead.

I consider myself to have pretty thick skin, but in the days and months that followed our failed IVF news, I felt so fragile. Like a porcelain doll that could be shattered into a million pieces by the smallest movement. And then there was the draining emotional effort that it took to be around people. Every moment I was in public felt like a war to fight back tears. My grief was still too fresh, and I needed more time to come to terms with the loss I had just suffered.

I didn't hear much from Becky for about a month. Then I received a text from her asking if we could go to dinner. My heart sunk. I knew exactly what the purpose of this dinner was, and I also knew myself well enough to know that I couldn't handle a big, public reveal. I wanted to hear the news from her, but privately. I needed simple and safe, where I felt the freedom to cry if I needed to. I wanted to hug her neck and, through tears, tell her I was happy for her.

I wrote her back and told her that I had a feeling I knew what she was going to tell me and asked if she could just come over. She was offended that I wasn't able to rejoice with her like she wanted me to. And I didn't have the words yet to explain why I couldn't. I didn't know how to describe the grief I was feeling to Becky or anyone else who had never felt a loss like that. Unfortunately, that was the beginning of the slow death of my friendship with Becky. She was too consumed with joy to sit with me in my grief the way I needed her to, and I was

Rejoice with those who rejoice;
mourn with those who mourn.
Live in harmony with one another.

Romans 12:15–16

too consumed in my grief to partake in her joy like she wanted me to. We both made mistakes. We both could have handled the situation a whole lot better. Neither of us gave each other nearly enough grace.

MENDING FENCES

A huge part of living a life of grace is apologizing when you've wronged someone and forgiving when someone has wronged you. Not every failing friendship can be saved with an apology, but making it up to someone when we've been wrong is good for our hearts. It's never too late to reach out and tell someone that you are sorry that you hurt her. I did apologize to Becky and she apologized to me. I've forgiven her, and I hope she's forgiven me. But our friendship was never the same after that, and I've given us both grace enough for that to be okay.

So, while your apology might be the catalyst to save a friendship, it might not. Pray about it and listen to God to find the right moment. Then, all you can do is accept responsibility for your actions, genuinely apologize, truly forgive, and offer grace moving forward. You can't control whether or not she wants to move forward. Either way, accept it with grace and a now lighter heart!

It's a horrible feeling to know that a friendship was lost because of a lack of grace. I spent the next year trying to figure out how to put into words how the whole process made me feel, how it had changed me. I carried around so much sadness over how things had gone with Becky. I was happy for her. But I couldn't pretend that I wasn't also sad for me. When it came down to it, Becky didn't want her joy to be marred by my grief. She wanted her friend to happily follow along with her journey, help throw her a baby shower, and squeal over her gender reveal. But I couldn't do all of that then, when my grief was so fresh and raw. I could not watch her receive the very thing I'd prayed for so diligently without sadness for me tinging my joy for her. I felt horribly that I wasn't able to be there for her in the way she would have liked.

Romans 12:15 says, "Rejoice with those who rejoice; mourn with those who mourn." I wrestled with this verse a lot. I can't even count the times that it was quoted to me, almost as if it was being thrown in my face. Yes, this verse is a call to celebrate with people who are experiencing joy. And I believe wholeheartedly that we are supposed to rejoice when good things happen to others. The part that I have had a hard time with is the unrealistic expectation the world places on people concerning what rejoicing should look like. I believe we can rejoice for others through the tears over our own story, feeling intense grief over our own circumstances while also rejoicing. But that does not mean pretending that we aren't grieving. It does not mean shoving our feelings down and putting on a happy face to make someone else feel more comfortable.

To find peace as my heart healed, I had to give myself some serious grace. After a lot of prayer, I came to the conclusion that grief and joy can absolutely coexist. They are not mutually exclusive. It's okay to be sad for me and happy for her. Being sad over my story did not mean I wasn't happy for how hers was being written. But it takes understanding on both sides and a willingness to be unselfish for relationships to work in the middle of grief.

It was easy for me to blame Becky for what had happened, but the truth is that our friendship ended because we were both selfish. Becky didn't know how to be there for me, so she turned inward and focused on herself instead. I didn't know how to be there for her, so I turned inward and focused on myself. I had high expectations for how a friend should mourn with me. And she had high expectations for how a friend should rejoice with her. Neither of us could have anticipated that we would be mourning and rejoicing at the same time over the same things.

I can only control my choices, my actions, and my expectations for others. I can't control others' expectations of me. I can't control others' unwillingness to set their joy aside momentarily

The LORD is close to the brokenhearted and saves those who are crushed in spirit.

Psalm 34:18

while I grieve. I can't control others' lack of understanding when my rejoicing looks different during a heartbreaking season. And that's okay. My happiness and joy over someone else's blessings might not look the way they expect it to, but I can't control that. I can only work to understand, appreciate, and celebrate, in my own way, others' seasons of joy.

It doesn't matter if you are sitting on the side of grief or on the side of joy. I encourage you to let go of unrealistic expectations of yourself and others. There are times when you have to be willing to let your heart and your feelings take a back seat for a bit, so that you can meet people where they are and be there for them. Give your people grace as they join you to mourn or rejoice. They will bring whatever they can to the table. It might not feel like enough, but if you are willing to create a space for joy and grief to coexist, I truly believe God will make up the difference.

Stop and Reflect

Have you had a time with a friend when your expectations of each other came between you?

_____

_____

_____

Were you able to bridge the gap?

The righteous choose
their friends carefully,
but the way of the wicked
leads them astray.

Proverbs 12:26

If not, can you look back on it now and see where you both could have given each other more grace?

_____

_____

_____

_____

_____

_____

_____

_____

_____

_____

_____

When a friendship lets you down or dies a slow death like mine did, our natural response is to protect our hearts. I withdrew from so many of my friends as I tried to heal my heart and mourn after our first IVF attempt. I thought I was making things easier on myself, but I was really making things so much harder. Yes, there were some friends like Becky, who could not wrap their heads around what I was experiencing. But there were other friends that 100% had my back and wanted to be there for me, but I often wouldn't let them.

We need our people in all seasons, but we really need them when life gets hard. Blake and I were terrified to share our infertility story because we had no idea what people would say. Early on in our marriage, we were scared to share that we were going through a rough patch because we didn't know how people would respond. While there are challenges that come with letting people in, the good far outweighs the bad. Our friendships can lift us up, encourage us when we falter, see us clearly when we can't, and cover us in grace when our own wells run dry.

Receiving grace can be, at times, more difficult than giving it to others. When we feel at our lowest, our smallest, our meanest, well, that's when we need grace the most. But that's also when we feel we deserve it the least. When I failed to get pregnant even after treatment, I felt so broken. I felt like a failure, undeserving, unlovable.

Luckily, I had friends who offered grace again and again until I was ready to take it. They called and texted and kept calling and texting even when I didn't answer. They kept showing up even when I tried to push them away. They got into the mess with me. They listened. They held me and let me cry. Their presence and the grace that came with it slowly helped me bandage my wounds, stand up, and keep going.

I've got some good news for you. You get to choose your people. The people who are stingy with grace? You don't have to keep letting them in. The people who show up in spades, ready to fight by your side? Ready to pray for you and be there for you? You get to let them. The people you choose become the biggest voices in your life. Their opinions should be ones you respect. Their advice should be sound and come from a place of love. Their relationships with God should be inspiring. Who are you going to allow to be the voices in your life? Make that decision. Make it prayerfully. Make it thoughtfully. Make it wisely.

The people who get to speak into your life should be the ones that see your life day in and day out. They should know your routines, your rhythms, your strengths and weaknesses, your personality, your goals, your spiritual journey, your wins and your losses, and they should love you through it all. Once you make this decision, you can set boundaries to keep your heart protected from those who don't uplift you or support the journey you're on. You get to walk in freedom because the whole world no longer gets to have a say in your life. Your people do. That's it.

People can make life tricky, but they can also make life so sweet. Decide who your people are going to be and let them in. Be vulnerable. Show them your heart. Tell them where you are struggling most so that they can pray with you and for you. Surround yourself with people who take their struggles and heartache to God in prayer, people who are excellent listeners, and people who are willing to roll up their sleeves and do life alongside you, even when it's messy. People who will mourn with you when you mourn and rejoice with you when you rejoice, no matter what that looks like.

Let's Pray

Dear God,

Please show me who my people are. Help me to find friends and mentors who are filled with Your grace and Your love and are happy to share both. Help me to realize when I'm not being the friend that I should be to others and then help me to find a way to do better.

In Your Son's name, amen.

TWELVE

Grace in friendship

—

When Blake and I had moved to Auburn, I was working full time in pharmaceutical sales. I started my business called Scarlet & Gold as a creative outlet and as a side hustle for extra money. I worked with a graphic designer to create branding and artwork that we could feature on wall art. When I first opened, the business received approximately twenty orders a month, and I packaged every print by hand, tied beautiful gold ribbon around each black box, and wrote a handwritten thank-you note to each and every customer.

As we approached Christmas, I wanted to put together a Christmas-themed wall art collection. Our designer was busy with other projects, so she sent me the recommendation of a girl she'd worked with at a branding agency. Her name was Koral, and she said I'd love her.

Fast forward almost seven years, and Koral is my very best friend. We have walked through a whole lot of life together. We've endured seasons of business that were out of this world and seasons of business when we had no money coming in and no direction or ideas on how we could turn it around. We walked through Koral's pregnancy while I was in the thick of my infertility journey. I was by her side as she navigated the new world of motherhood, and she wiped my tears when I found out our first round of IVF failed. She held me up on my darkest days of grief, she gave me space when I needed it, and she pushed me when she knew I was ready to try again.

Koral, Jesus, and the prayers of a community are the reasons my boys are here. We wanted to try again, but we couldn't afford it. Koral worked with our team to organize, fund, and produce a collection of products that we called The Give Grace Campaign. The products in this collection were funded by my team, inspired by my story, and all the proceeds went to cover the expenses of our second round of IVF. I shared our infertility story publicly for the first time when we launched this campaign. I'll never forget all the people who rallied around us to pray, buy products, and encourage us on our journey, all because of Koral.

After the money was raised and the plans were set for us to travel to Denver, Koral drove down to Auburn for a photoshoot. After we wrapped up shooting, we finally had some time, just the two of us, and I could tell something was off. She took a deep breath, sat down beside me, and said, "I have to tell you something." As tears streamed down her face, she mustered up the courage to say, "I'm pregnant." Her pregnancy was a total surprise, and she was so worried about my heart. Here she was experiencing the greatest joy, but she was consumed by how it would make me feel. She grabbed my hand

A friend loves at all times,
and a brother is born
for a time of adversity.

Proverbs 17:17

and said, "This is supposed to be your time. I am supposed to be there for you like you were there for me."

And she was.

Every step of the way she had and continues to be there for me. She has loved me, supported me, protected my heart, and fought for our friendship. Her pregnancy could have put a strain on our relationship, but instead it brought us closer together. I have learned a lot from my friend Koral over the past seven years about doing life with someone and how to give grace through the good days and the hard days. We've walked through a lot of storms, celebrated a lot of accomplishments, and navigated a lot of new roads together. Our friendship has stood the test of time and lots of trials because we've been able to give each other lots of grace as we let go of the small things and fought to hold each other up when we needed it most.

Stop and Reflect

Do you have a friend like Koral?

_____

_____

_____

_____

_____

What makes her such a great friend?

_____

_____

_____

_____

_____

_____

_____

_____

_____

How can you be more like her in all of your friendships?

_____

_____

_____

_____

_____

_____

_____

_____

_____

Perfume and incense bring
joy to the heart, and
the pleasantness of
a friend springs from
their heartfelt advice.

Proverbs 27:9

People can complicate life, hurt us, fail us, stab us in the back, and say all the wrong things. They might let us down and disappoint us, but they also bring so much beauty to life. They pray for us, lift us up when we are too weary to take the next step, speak wise words into our circumstances, and walk through our mess with us.

When you put two imperfect people together in friendship or in marriage, heartache will happen at some point. Koral has taught me that living in community means that you should always start by seeking to understand. When someone has really hurt her, let her down, or treated her poorly, Koral immediately tries to put herself into that person's shoes. Koral never walked through infertility. She didn't know exactly what I was feeling, but she always tried to understand. She researched what I was going through. She asked me questions. She validated my feelings when I needed it most. She always recognized that she didn't understand my exact pain, but her actions made it clear that she understood pain and that she was seeking to try to understand in any way that she could.

One night Koral and I were at my house. Maison (her oldest) was a baby, and she was trying to get her to sleep. I was having an emotional day and pouring out all my feelings to Koral as she was nursing and rocking her baby.

Koral's first-time mom stress was probably off the charts, but I never felt that from her. I never felt like I was an inconvenience to her bedtime routine. She could have pushed me off because it wasn't a good time. She could have asked me to talk about this later, but she knew I needed her. So she met me right there, got in my mess (emotionally speaking), listened, and helped me sort through all that I was feeling. It was a simple moment. She probably doesn't even remember it, but it meant a lot to me. It taught me the importance of stopping what I'm doing to love on my people when they need me most.

Sometimes we pack our lives and schedules so full that we don't have time to slow down, stop, and be there for our people. I know I am guilty of that. Koral has shown me the value of slowing down and making time to be there for people when they need me. I've learned how to be present. Our people just need us to have the grace to meet them where they are. They need us to show up, wrap our arms around their necks, dry their tears, listen, and be still. Together.

My experiences with two very different friends, Koral and Becky, during the hardest season of my life so far have taught me a lot about friendship. The types of friendships I want to have and the type of friend I want to be. What kind of friend do you want to be? I want to be the kind of friend who shows up for my people. I want to be the kind of friend who reaches out, even when I have no idea what to say. I want to be the kind of friend who apologizes quickly when I say the wrong thing and learns from my mistakes. I want to be the kind of friend who's willing to roll up my sleeves and jump headfirst into the good, the bad, and the ugly of my friends' lives. I want to be the type of friend who loves people through the fullness of grace that flows from my heart. And that's the type of friend I want to have too!

LISTENING EARS

I listened to an episode of Emily P. Freeman's podcast, *The Next Right Thing*, and she talked about a listening exercise she participated in as part of a retreat. Someone sat in the hot seat and this person was "the talker." Everyone else was to listen with these guidelines: Don't make a statement. Don't quote Scripture. Don't offer to pray. The only thing the listeners were allowed to do was ask questions. The first person got in the hot seat, and Emily struggled not to give compelling advice, relate the speaker's story to her story, or to give comfort and perspective. It was a challenge for Emily to just listen instead of speak.

As a listener, Emily described the experience as very unsatisfying because she felt like she hadn't helped the person. But the person sitting in the hot seat looked relieved. When it was Emily's turn, she shared a story and the listeners asked a first, second, and third question. When her time was up, Emily realized no one had offered any advice, answers, solutions, or personal anecdotes. However, she described feeling more understood and cared for than she ever had been when it came to this particular situation.

Wow! What if instead of interjecting yourself into the situation, you listened and gave people the space to think about and process how they're feeling? Try it. I think you'll be amazed at what it does for your friendships.

To be that type of friend you have to be willing to show up, willing to listen with your whole heart, willing to be honest and communicate your needs clearly, and willing to let love and grace take precedence over judgement and the need to be right. I learned that my relationships are better when I communicate where I am emotionally and what I need from my people. When I let them off the hook and stop expecting them to just know, life goes a lot smoother. Over the years, I've been able to avoid conflict, unmet expectations, and hurt feelings by simply expressing my needs up front. This takes the guessing game out of the equation and allows your people to love you better.

Listening is a true art, one that Koral excels at. She doesn't try to fix things. She doesn't one up me. She doesn't offer unsolicited advice. She doesn't act like an expert in whatever subject matter I'm discussing. She doesn't throw Scripture at me when I'm trying to process. She simply listens. Luckily, listening is a skill that can be learned. We become good listeners by disciplining ourselves to ask a question and then a second question and sometimes even a third question before we speak. Sometimes grace doesn't say a word. Sometimes grace simply listens and lets God do the speaking.

Genuine and authentic friendship will bless your life in a big way. Friends like Koral are worth fighting for and going the extra mile for. And they will do the same for you. Don't give up until you find a friend like this. You deserve it and she does too. We may not know what others are walking through. We might not have a clue what their pain feels like. We might not know what to say, and that's okay. You're not supposed to have the answers. You're simply supposed to show up, seek to understand, be vulnerable, meet people where they are, and listen. Let's give grace freely to others because it's first been given to us.

Let's Pray

Father God,

Thank You for genuine friendship. The friends You have sent me are so valuable, and I am so grateful for their love and grace in my life. Help me to find and build a vibrant community of friends like these. Help me to be a friend worth having to my people.

In Your Son's name, amen.

THIRTEEN

Give grace freely

—

I want to leave a legacy that goes far beyond stuff. When I get to the end of my life, I want to look back and be proud of how I loved people. How I gave grace freely and with joy. I want to rest in the knowledge that I took care of people's hearts. I want to leave people better than I found them.

If you want to leave an impact on the world, you have to start with one person. Sometimes we allow our big dreams and aspirations to stop us in our tracks because they feel so daunting. When we look at the big picture, it can be overwhelming to think about getting from point A to point B. Luckily, legacies are built over time. They are built by being faithful with what's in front of us. They are built one person at a time, one interaction at a time.

I love Dave Ramsey's "Momentum Theorem." It says: "Focused intensity over time multiplied by God leads to unstoppable momentum." I want to run after loving others and pouring out grace on every person I meet with focused intensity. Why? Because it matters for the kingdom. Pouring into others, even with something as simple as an encouraging word to the cashier at the grocery store, is an eternal investment.

For no one can lay
any foundation other
than the one already laid,
which is Jesus Christ.

1 Corinthians 3:11

God uses the tiny seeds of faithfulness that we plant to change the course of lives.

None of us have earned God's grace. It's actually the opposite of what we deserve. So who are we to hold onto grace and not extend it to others? To love people well, we must give grace away freely, even when it's undeserved. This isn't always easy, and, more often than not, it's downright difficult. But it's still worth doing, difficult or not.

Maybe you're a little like me. I'm great at giving grace to people who are nice to me. I'm even decent at giving grace to a rude or grumpy stranger. But I really struggle giving grace to people who have caused a deep wound in my heart. I have a hard time getting past the betrayal and my belief, fair or not, that they should have known better. Or even worse, when I know that they *did* know better and still chose to hurt me.

However, holding onto grace tightly, and only giving it those we believe deserve it, is not the answer. Grace, by its very nature, is meant to be shared freely, with abandon. At those times when I don't want to give even a little, God reminds me that I too know better and have, at times, chosen to hurt others. I've chosen my own way over His. But no matter how many times I stray or choose my own desires over obedience, God meets me with grace, mercy, forgiveness, and open arms. That is why we have to do the same for others. We give grace away freely because He first gives it to us.

NEW GRACE FOR OLD HURTS

We all have old hurts and heartbreaks that can hold us back. Fear of rejection left over from a friend who turned on us. A wall around our heart built after a love ghosted us. An old, still aching bruise to our pride after we didn't get into that prestigious school or internship or land that dream job. It's time to give ourselves and others grace for these lingering hurts.

If someone wronged you and you are still holding onto it, it's time to forgive. I want you to write him or her a letter, sharing all of your feelings and tell them that you forgive them. Hold onto that letter and read it to yourself each day until you actually do feel forgiveness in your heart. Then, if you want to, you can send the letter. But you don't have to.

And if you've wronged someone and it still haunts you? Well, it's time to apologize. She may not be ready to give grace and forgive you, but once you genuinely say that you are sorry and do your best to make it up to her, you can start the work of forgiving yourself. Forgiveness is a key component of grace, and we can't do the necessary work of healing without it.

Sometimes it's the people you least expected who love you the most when things get tough. Remember the people who have lived out grace for you when you needed it the most. These grace givers are the people who you want to build a community with. They are the ones who will hold you accountable, lead you gently back to Jesus when you have strayed, and love you at your most unlovable. The grace givers in your life are blessings worth thanking God for each and every day.

I've been loved really well by my village, and I've taken notes along the way so that I can do the same in return for my people. Not sure how to start giving grace? Think back to something someone did that had a big positive impact on your heart. How can you do that for someone else? When someone does something nice for you, I encourage you to write it down somewhere. This will help you make a point to remember how it made you feel. Do that for someone in your life who could use a little more grace.

When I was in my darkest season of infertility, I used to go over to my neighbors' house and hang out with her and her two daughters a lot. I would play with the kids, help with dinner, help with bath and bedtime, and just get to be a part of their family for a little while. This time helped give me a sense of purpose to the waiting for an unknown future. Spending time there was healing for my heart. For a brief moment in time, I was able to forget about what we were walking through and help take care of those sweet girls. It allowed me an opportunity to serve, even if I was simply an extra set of hands. Serving

Very truly I tell you, no servant is greater than his master, nor is a messenger greater than the one who sent him. Now that you know these things, you will be blessed if you do them."

John 13:16–17

and loving them allowed me to take my eyes off my heartache for a bit.

I know that so much of my healing happened in the moments when I got outside of myself and my circumstances to help someone else. When you step outside of yourself, your eyes are opened to life beyond your circumstances. It helps put whatever you are going through into perspective. Helping others gives you a sense of purpose, belonging, and satisfaction.

How can you serve others? There are lots of ways! You can serve others by offering your time, your resources, or your gifts. God has given each one of us unique gifts that are all our own. Maybe you've been overthinking your gifts and feel stuck because you don't know *how* to use them. Or maybe you aren't completely sure what your gifts are. There are multiple online tests you can take to help you assess your gifts, but you can also talk to the people around you who are able to see you in ways you cannot see yourself. It's really a simple question: what do you have in abundance that you can share with someone else?

If you are an excellent cook, make dinner for a friend who is struggling, or drop off one of your famous pies for your pastor. Are you an organizational whiz with time to share? Look for a local charity that could use your skills, or volunteer to help a friend get organized after a move! Have you been blessed with your finances? Gently see if anyone you know is in need. An anonymous gift from you could make a big difference. Or make a bigger-than-usual donation to your favorite charity or your church. Maybe your gift is that you're a fantastic listener or a prayer warrior. What might seem simple to you may mean a whole lot to the person you're helping. My mom always says that laundry is one of her spiritual gifts, and she loves using it to serve her kids. And I'm not going to lie, I love that she loves laundry, because I do not!

Simple acts of service and kindness go a long way. There are countless ways to inject a little more grace and love into the world. Your way of giving grace will be as unique as you are. Follow your heart and listen for little whispers from God to direct your steps for where your special brand of grace is most needed.

When we look at the life of Jesus, He was all about serving people. At the Last Supper, the last thing Jesus did with His disciples was to wash their feet. In His last few moments on Earth, Jesus could have done anything, but He *chose* to humble Himself to the level of a servant and wash His disciples' feet. It's a powerful illustration to see how God views the importance of serving. If Jesus can do that, so can we. We must lower and humble ourselves, look for ways to serve, and walk in with a willing heart.

Stop and Reflect

Who could use a little more grace in your life?

_____

_____

_____

What are some gifts you can share or ways you can serve them to give them that grace?

_____

_____

_____

How can you use your gifts to serve your community more regularly?

_____

_____

_____

Want another way to spread some grace? Everyone needs a hype squad. No matter what kind of day I'm having, encouragement from others means so much to me. It's always nice to hear I am loved, I am doing a good job, or someone is proud of me. Words of affirmation is one of my love languages, so encouraging words from others mean a lot to me.

Words have power. They have the power to build people up or tear them down. They have the power to give grace or break hearts. Words can change the trajectory of someone's day for better or for worse in a matter of minutes. We have to be careful with how we use our words. We can use them wisely or carelessly. If we mess up, we can apologize, we can explain, but, once spoken, we can never take them back.

I want to bless others with my words. I want to be slow to speak so that I can be intentional with my words. I want to speak life over my kids. I want to tell them every single day that I love them. The more we have grace spoken over us, the more equipped we feel to tackle any obstacle in front of us. I try to encourage someone with my words every single day. Some days I focus on my kids and husband, or the people I encounter over the course of my day like the pharmacist, the checkout girl at the grocery, or my UPS guy. But other days, when I have more time, I will put a letter in the mail, send a quick text, leave a voicemail, write an email, or tell someone I love in person. I send verses, tell them what they mean to me, tell them why I'm proud of them, tell them why I think they are doing a great job, or just speak hope over them. This takes me so little time, but I can't tell you how many friends have texted me back or said, "You have no idea how much I needed to hear this today!" Knowing that I brightened someone's day with my words blesses me as much or more as it blesses whomever I'm sending it to.

Therefore encourage one another and build each other up, just as in fact you are doing.

1 Thessalonians 5:11

Sharing encouragement with others fills our hearts with joy. It helps us focus on things we are grateful for and makes us think about why we love the people around us. Being an encourager is a way of sharing grace with others, and it's not too late to start this practice today.

Encouraging someone isn't just done with words, although that's an excellent place to start. Blake encourages me every day with acts of service. He's always doing little things that make my life easier and better. And I have a friend who finds the absolute perfect gifts. She seems to file away every small comment and conversation and always manages to give me (and all of our other friends) exactly what we've been needing or wanting. I am always encouraged by her gifts because they make me feel so *known*. I have another friend who encourages by showing up. She sacrifices her time freely to be there for others, no matter how much she has going on personally. And my little guys encourage me every day, even on the hardest days of motherhood, with their hugs and kisses and the way they slide their little hands in mine. No matter what your personal love language is, you can use it to encourage others.

There's something powerful and motivating about watching or hearing about someone else face and overcome an obstacle. Does watching someone else walk through the darkness and come into the light give you encouragement? Does it make you feel like you can overcome too?

My favorite part of these stories of success are when people take what they have learned back to their communities and use it to help others. The tools gained in the process of overcoming obstacles now become tools that anyone can use. When we share what grace has done in our lives and how God has helped us tackle life's tough stuff, we can help others avoid the pitfalls and mistakes we made. Sharing is a form of grace in and of itself.

You are the hero of your story, just like I'm the hero of mine. When you walk through hard things in life and stand on the other side in victory, you have a choice to make. You can keep your stories to yourself, filled with anger, bitterness, or shame, because you had to go through something difficult or embarrassing. Or you can choose grace and choose to share.

You can choose to take what you've learned, integrate it into your life, and allow it to change your perspective. You can choose to let it help you to grow, become more compassionate, more humble, more empathetic, more joyous, and a whole lot stronger. You can use your growth to impact others around you. How? By teaching, by simply living with less judgement and more compassion, by knowing how to help others who are fighting the same battle, and by giving grace freely to yourself and to those around you.

Our stories shape us. Our hardships define us. We get to choose what to do with that. Our testimony has the power to transform hearts. Humans are story-driven beings, and our testimony about God's faithfulness in our lives is one of the most impactful tools we have in sharing the gospel. People connect with stories. They listen to them. And they will find themselves in *your* story, if you let them. When you share your story with others and talk about how God was real and faithful to you through good days and bad days, it gives others hope that this same God will be real to them too. Your story is too powerful to keep it to yourself. Give it away and watch what God does with it.

Let's Pray

Father God,

Show me clearly all the ways that Your grace has transformed my story. Help me to share all of that honestly with those who need to hear it. Help me to be brave and unashamed as I share my mistakes and missteps and help them to hear clearly when I tell of Your love, kindness, and wisdom.

In Jesus' name, amen.

Conclusion

Grace is truly amazing isn't it? A miracle that none of us deserve, but that we are all blessed to receive. It holds so much potential for empathy, healing, and comfort. It calls out to each of us, beckoning us to accept it for ourselves and share it freely with others.

I hope that my story has helped you see how big a role grace can have in each of our stories. We will all walk through dark times that feel too difficult to bear, we will all mess up and desperately need forgiveness, and we will all do things that leave us feeling ashamed or stupid or small. And those things aren't a matter of *if*, but *when*. Life is hard, but grace is the balm that we all need during those times.

I wish I could hold your hand through it all. But, luckily, even during the times you might feel most alone, you never are. God is always with us. Even when we turn away from Him, curse His name, or unload our anger at His feet, God will never leave us. His love for us will never fade or falter. His grace will never stop covering us. How lucky are we?

I want to encourage you to look around your life and see how you can intentionally give grace the way that God does.

Now I commit you to God and to the word of his grace, which can build you up and give you an inheritance among all those who are sanctified.

Acts 20:32

Grace that truly listens instead of rushing in to talk. Grace that celebrates our differences instead of erasing them. Grace that validates our feelings instead of judging them. Grace that forgives, even when we don't deserve it. Grace that loves us at our worst. Grace that heals the deep wounds and smooths out our old scars. Grace that helps us find new ways forward together.

If we could all do that, can you imagine how our world would change for the better? How much more love and understanding there would be? Grace has always been the secret key to connecting deeply with one another, so let's use it. Unlock your doors and windows and throw them open wide, let God's grace stream out through you to anyone who needs it and everyone who wants it. When you let grace out, you also open the door for grace to come in. Funny how that works, isn't it? The more you give, the more you receive, and the more you receive, the more you have to give. So go out there and live a life with abundant grace by giving grace however and whenever you can. I'll be cheering you on the whole way!